PENGUIN BUSI

KARMA SUTRAS

Debashis Chatterjee has taught leadership classes at Harvard University and at the Indian Institute of Management (IIM) Calcutta, Lucknow and Kozhikode for three decades. He has been awarded the prestigious Fulbright Fellowship twice for pre-doctoral and postdoctoral work at the Kennedy School of Government at Harvard University. His published works include eighteen books, such as *Leading Consciously* (foreword by Peter M. Senge) and *Timeless Leadership*. He published his debut novel, *Krishna: The 7th Sense*, in 2022. His books have been translated in several Indian and international languages. He has trained more than hundred thousand managers globally in Fortune 500 corporations and over sixty thousand school principals and teachers. He has served as a leadership coach to prominent political leaders and CEOs of major Indian organizations. He has also served as a dean of an international business school in Singapore. A pioneer in the field of Asian models in leadership, Chatterjee served as the director of the IIM Kozhikode for two terms (2009–2023) and as dean and tenured professor at IIM Lucknow. He is credited with transforming IIM Kozhikode from an obscure regional school to an institution of national impact and global recognition. He also served as the director general of IMI, Delhi, India's first corporate sponsored business school, and as independent director on the boards of several multinational and Indian companies. Debashis Chatterjee was the mentor director of IIM Amritsar from June 2018 to July 2019. He was reappointed as the director of IIM Kozhikode for a third five-year term in 2023. He can be reached at:

Email: dciiml@gmail.com
LinkedIn: https://www.linkedin.com/in/debashischatterjee1

Celebrating 35 Years of
Penguin Random House India

Karma Sutras

Leadership
and Wisdom in
Uncertain Times

Debashis Chatterjee

Series Editor

PENGUIN
BUSINESS

An imprint of Penguin Random House

PENGUIN BUSINESS

USA | Canada | UK | Ireland | Australia
New Zealand | India | South Africa | China | Singapore

Penguin Business is part of the Penguin Random House group of companies
whose addresses can be found at global.penguinrandomhouse.com

Published by Penguin Random House India Pvt. Ltd
4th Floor, Capital Tower 1, MG Road,
Gurugram 122 002, Haryana, India

First published by SAGE Publications India Pvt Ltd 2021
Published in Penguin Business by Penguin Random House India 2023

ISBN 9780143461753

Typeset in 10/14pt ITC Stone Serif by Fidus Design Pvt Ltd, Chandigarh

www.penguin.co.in

Dedicated to

*the PGP class of 1995
at IIM Calcutta,*

the class of 1998 at IIM Lucknow,

*the class of 2019 at
IIM Amritsar and*

*my faculty colleagues at
IIM Kozhikode*

*for letting me know that leadership
cannot be taught until it is learnt!*

CONTENTS

FOREWORD

It has been almost two years since a thoughtful young professor of management from India visited me at Massachusetts Institute of Technology (MIT) and commented, 'What is oldest is often most valuable. When an idea has persisted for thousands of years, we can have some confidence in its truth.' That thoughtful young man Debashis Chatterjee has now completed a book, and it is a very great privilege to be able to introduce it. In this book, he presents and explains diverse threads of ancient-wisdom teachings, relating these insights to the challenges of leading contemporary organizations. He does so with remarkable clarity, simplicity and persuasiveness. Ideas that might otherwise be regarded as hopelessly esoteric or impractical emerge as bedrock notions of what it means to lead and to work together effectively. Time-honoured philosophic perspectives illuminate why work in one setting evokes passion, imagination and genuine commitment, while all three are absent in another. In doing so, I find that this book speaks more directly to the crucial problems which afflict contemporary organizations than most 'how to' management nostrums. 'If a person rises to a level of authority that exceeds his virtue, all will suffer,' wrote Guanzi, a predecessor of Confucius, 2,500 years ago. Is there any reason to think this advice less relevant today than when it was written, especially in the era of enterprises which influence the lives of people around the world? How many suffer, both inside organizations and beyond, from abuse of power, leadership lacking wisdom and deep understanding, and decisions based on shallow, frenzied thinking, which nonetheless affect thousands? Was this only a problem relevant 2,500 years ago? Or are we, if anything, more in need now than ever before of a set of guiding precepts to aid in the formation of leaders, so that power would be in balance with virtue? If so, why is this problem virtually ignored and all the attention is paid to high performance, world-class competition and leading global enterprises? I think there are two reasons. First, it is not actually the vision we are following. Balancing power with virtue actually runs counter to our more accepted assumptions that people rise to positions of authority because of their competence, technical skill or proven ability to produce results. In fact, this itself is a rather rosy picture. In point of fact, many rise to positions of power because that is their ambition, they know how to make impressions and they are masters at the internal political game playing that dominates most large enterprises. Second, even if we embrace the vision that power and virtue should go together, we have little idea how to pursue such a vision. We have agreed upon a set of guiding ideas as to what constitutes virtue. We have no shared understanding of how virtue and wisdom develop in a person throughout their life. We all recognize the difference between espousing laudable values and practising those values. But we have little shared understanding of why one person has developed integrity and another has not. The result is that many in positions of authority lack the capabilities to truly lead. They are not credible. They do not command genuine respect. They are not committed to serve. They are not continually learning and growing. They are not wise. As Debashis Chatterjee shows, ancient traditions like those of India and China have something important to contribute to understanding true leadership development. The cultivation of virtue, they believed, followed from the development of consciousness. Development, Chatterjee points out, has the same root as an envelope. It literally means 'de-enveloping' or opening up. As a human being opens up, their awareness expands to embrace more and more complexities of life, the realities of their organization and the principles of nature.

Higher virtues are at some elemental level nothing more or less than deeply appreciating laws of nature that enable harmony and functioning of life—see reality as it is (commitment to the truth), take no more than you need (waste not, want not), do not control unnecessarily (hierarchical power should be used only when local solutions are not possible, what 17th-century philosophers called the principle of 'subsidiarity') and balance action with non-action (the power of presence, true listening and non-intervention). Internalizing such virtues that do not come from 'the outside in' taught to us as moral codes that must be followed blindly. These are virtues that we experience and follow naturally as our consciousness opens up, de-envelops. This constitutes a very different approach to leadership development than practised in most contemporary organizations. It is neither quick nor simple. It demands deep commitment and disciplined practice. It is no 'flavour of the month' management fad; its merits have been proven, literally, over thousands of years. The implications of this book stretch beyond development of hierarchical leaders. Successful enterprises of the coming millennium may find that leadership is too important to be reserved for a few. Leadership comes in many shapes and sizes, only one type of which concerns people in positions of authority. It is not a hyperbole to think of 'leadership organizations' as organizations of leaders, for the principles and practices of developing apply to all people. As more and more managers come to understand the importance of growth of people in order to grow as an enterprise, there will be increasing interest in more powerful theory and method for developing people. Rather than being a peripheral 'HR issue', growth of people and aligning their creative capacities is now a strategic imperative, perhaps 'the' strategic imperative, for many enterprises. No matter what is done in enterprises, it is done by people. The maturity and happiness of those people set the tone and determine the capabilities or limitations of that enterprise. We are leaving an era where great strides were made through developing and applying advanced knowledge in manufacturing, marketing and finance. These are now the price of admission to global markets. They no longer afford competitive advantage. We are entering an era, I believe, where world-class enterprises will build comparable sophistication in understanding and tapping the intelligence and spirit of human beings. This is why I expect this book to be a landmark in the journey towards cultivating the human side of enterprise. In the increasingly global business environment, it is just a matter of time before Western managers recognize the unique storehouse of practical knowledge about consciousness that resides in Eastern cultures, and before their Eastern counterparts rediscover it. Debashis Chatterjee's vision of offering ancient insights in a way that makes them understandable to contemporary managers could not be more timely. In an era entranced by 'the new', our greatest hope, ironically, may lie in rediscovering 'the old'. No one has yet been able to improve upon love nor find a technological substitute for joy or serenity. It is not that ancient wisdom is sacrosanct, nor that all answers to life's mysteries were revealed by India's Vedic sages. Rather, I see Debashis' most central message as really an invitation. Do we wish to rejoin an ancient line of enquiry? Do we wish to, once again, focus our energies on understanding what it means to be alive, to be aware, and to understand the sources of health and well-being, generativeness and happiness? If the answer is yes, then it would be foolhardy, indeed, to ignore the foundations we might build on. They are present in all the great spiritual traditions of the world. But they are in many ways especially accessible in those settings, like India and China, where there has been some continuity of development, some preservation of not only the articulations of spiritual insight but of the

KARMA SUTRAS

practices as well. This is a precious book. I hope it finds its way into the hands of readers who are as committed to the future as is the author.

Peter M. Senge
MIT, Cambridge, Massachusetts

PREFACE

This book is for high-potential managers and leaders who step into the world of work, sometimes without knowing how to work. These talented men and women seem to scurry through workspaces like children playfully running their fingers over the keyboard of a piano, making discordant noises. They learn on the job through unforced errors and sometimes severe trials. I can't quite blame them as I did so as well when I was on probation in my first job. I fumbled and faltered in the first couple of managerial roles that I had in the beginning of my career. I understood precious little about organizational politics and became an unwitting victim of it. I did not know that jealousy was not just about sibling rivalry but a part and parcel of corporate life as well. I also had the misfortune of getting one of my bosses fired. How I wished then that I had a mentor who would guide me along the way!

As I matured, I took on several leadership roles including sitting on the board of an organization in which I once worked as a probationer. My modest successes were not truly mine. They were the result of insights and guidance I had received from stalwarts in my field. These were titans who would lend their shoulders for me to get a global perspective on leadership. I might as well have named this book *Teachings of the Titans*.

The book is divided into two distinct segments as indicated by the title. These segments are Karma and Sutras. The first part is about the context of the word 'karma'. Contrary to popular belief, karma is not about fatalistic action. It is the broader and invisible context in which work takes place. Karma includes will, thought, intent and acts of omission as well as commission. They all create the large ecology of karma in which we find ourselves.

The second part is called sutras or insights. In Sanskrit, sutra means thread. Since 2005, I had written a very popular column in India's largest circulated newspaper. This column was called Success Sutras. A significant part of the second segment of this book has appeared in my work on *Leadership Sutras* (Chatterjee 2008). I added some new sutras and rewrote some more of them to suit the current context. These sutras provide deep insights into the art and practice of leadership from several thought leaders and spiritual traditions of the world.

This book is a treasure trove of simple but subtle ideas in the form of sutras. They were put together for over 25 years of my journey as an author, scholar and institution builder. I would suggest that you read the book in the same way that it was written—in silence and solitude. A certain receptivity and quietness of mind is required to come to terms with what the great masters of antiquity and the present are trying to convey to us through their lived lives and spoken words.

Leadership is not the privilege of a handful of high-flying executives. At its very best, it is a state of relationship between the leader and the led. A relationship cannot be possessed or dominated by a single person; it ceases to be a relationship then. This book recognizes that in each follower, there is an emerging leader. Leaders can lead because they are empowered by the spirit of followership. Here, I have tried to present not one model of leadership but several dimensions of followership that constitute a leader.

Each of us, consciously or unconsciously, has led in some field or another as parents, teachers, managers, doctors, athletes, entrepreneurs or even as students. In all these roles, we learn valuable lessons in leadership. I have as well. It is a privilege to pass on some of these lessons to you.

Those aspiring to lead organizations and institutions in the future may find a distant mentor when they read this book. I hope that insights of this book help them navigate the complex world of organizations going forward.

ACKNOWLEDGEMENTS

Knowledge belongs to finite time. What is infinite is ignorance. After writing this book, I realized how much I did not know about my own self. If I have anything in common with you, it is this ignorance. We all share ignorance in some form or the other. Even the wisest of human beings is not afraid to say, 'I do not know.'

So, I acknowledge, with humility, the many known and unknown sources of the knowledge contained in this book: my parents, grandmother, teachers and colleagues in three IIMs, especially the late Professor S. K. Chakraborty and Dr Pritam Singh two of my mentors—the sacred soil of India where I grew up and unknown co-travellers on my journeys around the world, who have all contributed to the unseen dimensions of this book.

My heartfelt gratitude to Peter Senge of MIT, who enabled me to dream of my first published work in the USA—*Leading Consciously*, the foundation on which *Karma Sutras* is based. The first part of the book builds on my conversations with several of my students in three IIMs and elsewhere and the leadership challenges they are likely to encounter. This work is an attempt to repay a part of my debt to my students who are now dispersed around the world.

A book project is an alchemy of collaboration. The alchemist is not necessarily the author. In this case, it is the editorial team who thought of this book as part of the SAGE–IIM Kozhikode Book Series that I was chosen to edit. I wish to acknowledge Manisha Mathews, Executive Editor, and Namarita Kathait, Associate Commissioning Editor, of SAGE, the two alchemists who brought this first book of the series to fruition. Their literary and publishing acumen has helped in the making of this book. I would like to express my deep gratitude to Mr Yohesh Srinivasan for lending me the craft of artist A. B. Biju, Payyanur, who did the illustrations for *Karma Sutras*.

I cannot forget to thank Sojan George, my executive secretary, for his constant support on the administrative front and Vaishnavi Nair, my research associate, who helped with the proofreading and compilation of the book.

Finally, Aditi, Shristi and Siddharth and our Labrador Mig, I am lucky to have had you around while this book was written. This writer's world would be a blank page without you.

Part 1
Karma

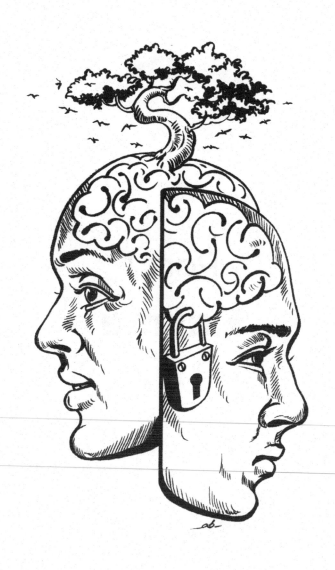

✳ **1** ✳

WISDOM OF UNCERTAINTY

Being at ease with not knowing is crucial for answers to come to you.

—Eckhart Tolle

THE NEW NORMAL

'What is happening to your business in these uncertain times?' I asked a retailer in the city.

'Don't ask me,' he said. 'Traditional retail is going downhill. People are distancing themselves socially. They are buying less from places that require community gathering. The global supply chain is disrupted. All the certainties of business are now gone.'

He then turned around and asked me, 'So, does one fix it all?'

I said, 'You can fix a product. But how can you fix a mindset that is not functioning? How do you fix your thinking in these turbulent times?'

'True, tell me more,' he said.

'Think of the word, "karma"', I said.

'That's so fatalistic!' he groaned!

'Karma has nothing to do with fate,' I said.

'Then, what does it mean?'

'It simply means conscious and thoughtful action.'

'Please explain more!'

'Karma does not mean fate. It is the context you find yourself in. The current situation you are facing in business is a result of your past thoughts. However, the future of your business will depend entirely on the quality of your actions in the present.'

'What is the first step towards conscious action?'

'The first step is to be conscious of an old mindset that you are carrying in your head about business as usual. Yet you can see that business as usual does not work anymore, just as business school as usual does not work for me anymore.'

'Why, what happened to the business school?' he queried.

I clarified, 'On-campus learning is turning out to be more expensive than online learning. Learning has broken tough old mindsets of space and time. Students do not want to learn within the limitations imposed by 90 minutes' periods. They want to learn in flexitime. Learning is turning out to be a function of human attention rather than a period of time. Likewise, learning is going to happen a lot less in a place called "the classroom" and a lot more in spaces that are digitally interconnected. It has moved from a physical class to a digital hub.'

'So how about the first step?'

'The first step is the most critical step, as the first button of your coat. If you get that wrong, the whole alignment of buttons is gone for a toss.'

'The first step is to be conscious of the old mindset about leading your enterprise that you are carrying inside your head. That is the old normal.'

'And what is the new normal?'

'The new normal is not sitting there like a target you have to hit. The new normal is what you create through your karma—your thoughtful and conscious action.'

I shared with him the following story to help navigate and lead in the world of uncertainty.

When businesses failed during the great depression, P&G came out of economic distress. They thought that soap is still an essential commodity in crisis while other companies cut costs for advertising. The president of P&G, at that time, Richard Dupree, in spite of objections from the shareholders, increased its advertising expenditure and came out of it unscathed. He actively pursued new marketing channels which, at the time, included the then rising commercial radio broadcasts that not only focused on the product but also the daily drama of people he imagined were like the people who bought P&G products. One of these campaigns involved becoming the chief sponsor of daytime serial dramas aimed at housewives—the company's primary market. The shows were associated with sponsors such as P&G's Oxydol, Duz and Ivory soaps and were dubbed 'soap operas'. In 1933, P&G debuted its first serial, Oxydol's Own Ma Perkins, and housewives around the country quickly fell in love with the daily stories. Similar daily serial dramas were created to bolster its other brands and, by 1939, the company was producing 21 of these so-called 'soap operas'. Thus, two industries were thriving due to the investments made by one.

Silicon Valley doesn't have better ideas and isn't smarter than the rest of the world, but it has the edge in filtering ideas and executing them.

—Sergey Brin, Google

FEWER TAKERS FOR TALENT, A LOT MORE FOR ATTITUDE

One of the insights that business leaders have often had is that talent is largely overrated. I agree. In times of uncertainty, where jobs are scarce, more and more talent will chase fewer jobs. Organizations that couldn't afford to hire very talented people will now not only be able to attract them for lesser salaries but also retain them longer because of job insecurity in the market.

But honestly, what will count in the long run is the kind of attitude talented employees bring to the enterprise. Think of a new generation of youngsters who have graduated through the COVID-19 world. This kind of graduation through the school of life has taught them many things that they wouldn't have learnt in a classroom. It has taught them the virtues of essentialism—emphasis on using minimum resources, conserving energy, saving more and consuming less.

The new attitude that generation Z will bring to the enterprise will shift businesses thinking from consuming to caring. This will have an impact on consumption patterns. The new generation will see attitudes shifting from the egocentric managerial world towards a more eco-centric, purposeful business. Businesses will be a lot more accountable for carbon footprints they leave behind. Enterprises will be hauled up more for outsourcing the social and environmental cost of doing business and making money.

Another attitudinal shift that will come about in organizations is the movement from the rigidity of structures and processes to flexibility and freedom to innovate. Leaders should give the graduates of the COVID-19 world the flexibility to manage their own time. This generation will work smarter and a lot harder if they have autonomy over the use of their time. At least, most of the generation tends to think that way.

Most talented, young managers come to an organization with a chip on their shoulders. Arrogance becomes their calling card. They become prisoners of what Stanford researcher Carol Dweck classifies as the 'fixed mindset'. Those with a fixed mindset believe that intelligence is a fixed commodity and does not change.

On the contrary, managers lesser in talent but greater in attitude become quick learners. They represent what Dweck describes as people with 'growth mindsets'. In times of uncertainty, the only way to grow is to accelerate the pace of learning. This requires an attitude of humility and an enduring belief that intelligence is not frozen but fluid in nature. Those with growth mindsets, according to Dweck, believe that intelligence can be enhanced with effort.

In the times of uncertainty, those with a growth mindset will be the ones who would survive and thrive.

Most people do not listen with an intent to understand; they listen with the intent to reply.

—Stephen R. Covey

HOW TO SHIFT YOUR ATTITUDE TOWARDS GROWTH MINDSET?

Three of the most unused critical tools in the arsenal for growth of new managers are listening, observing and failing.

Of the three, listening is the most important tool. Yet young managers get trained in big business schools in the art and practice of speaking well. Listening is a primary management tool, and it must be honed by every young manager aspiring to lead in their profession. Aytekin Tank, Founder at JotForm. com, describes how listening to his 4.1 million users inspired a new product idea. He does not sell online forms. He just helps a few million customers to run smarter and more productive businesses. In uncertain times, most managers have to listen to their customers' voices rather than their competition. They have to ask, 'What would make the customers' work life easier—on a daily, weekly, monthly or quarterly basis?' Then they create that product or service. My thumb rule is that young managers should adopt a listening to speaking ratio of 3:1. That is three times more listening than speaking.

Observation is the key to understanding the reality of what a customer wants. Observation leads to deeper insights and better ways of presenting a value proposition to customers. Tank wrote that growing up in his professional life, he was waiting in line at a sports shop renting out boats—kayaks and canoes—for recreation. He observed a prominently displayed message:

'We don't sell boats. We sell time on the water.'

His keen observation may have been the basis for his start-up. He looked into what customers really wanted when they were dealing with tedious form-filling: (a) relief from excessive information load and (b) stress reduction. That is exactly what Tank was selling to his customers through his successful company.

Finally, failing. Young managers do not realize that the more they succeed, the more they tend to repeat processes and tools they were successful with. In the age of uncertainty, this is a sure recipe for failure. What made you successful in the context of the past will fail you when the context has changed in the future. If using a hammer made you successful in breaking bricks, it does not necessarily mean that you should be using that hammer in extracting a painful tooth. A successful brick-breaker will end up being a failed dentist if they continue to use their hammer. In uncertain times, successful recipes of the past would work less and less. Young managers need to fail fast and fail forward to succeed.

THE FUNERAL OF MIDDLE MANAGEMENT

Most young managers hope to make it to the ranks of middle management sooner than later. With digital information systems fast changing the landscape of business decisions, middle managers themselves, as a species, are moving towards extinction. In turbulent times, organization leaders do not have the luxury of waiting for information to move up layers of hierarchy before they can act on that information.

The conventional definition of management is getting work done through people, but real management is developing people through work.

—Agha Hasan Abedi

Middle managers, by definition, inherit the task of command and control of information that emanates from line functions and pass them on to the top management. Traditional large organizations with businesses above five billion dollars had between 10 and 14 layers of hierarchy. In the volatile and uncertain world, we are in those organizational structures which will be as obsolete as dinosaurs were before extinction.

The command and control functions of middle management will be taken over by digital devices fuelled by artificial intelligence. Middle managers will be relegated to being digital pen pushers. Organizations will not employ middle managers just for screaming controlling messages to juniors, nor will they command respect based on their position in the hierarchy. The death of middle management, with the advent of sophisticated technology infrastructure, is now imminent. The only way middle managers can survive is by virtue of their expertise which cannot be substituted by machines anymore. In short, organizations will preside over the funeral of most middle managers in the times to come.

Young managers should not, therefore, inherit the old mindsets and bad habits of middle managers and face extinction themselves. They have to move from positional authority to performing power. They have to bring expertise on the table that top management will find valuable for strategizing and decision-making. In essence, they have to be catalysts for business and financial results. They have to be pillars supporting organizational leadership, not caterpillars eating away the vitality of the enterprise.

Elizabeth Lyle, leadership expert in Boston Consulting Group, quotes Warren Buffet who delivered a school lecture in which he said, 'The chains of habit are too light to be felt until they're too heavy to be broken.'

That's a very useful piece of advice for young managers who aspire to be leaders. As Buffet points out, the bad habits of old-era middle managers such as sticking to positional authority, not rocking the boat too much and endless meetings before and after meetings can get young talent into serious trouble going forward. Uncertain times call for questioning old assumptions, taking decisions based on partial or even incomplete information and constant awareness of the winds of change in and around the organization. These are some of the important 21st-century skills for young managers that are essential to their relevance and success in contemporary organizations.

LEADERS DON'T HIT TARGETS; THEY GROW PEOPLE WHO HIT TARGETS

In business, there is no escape from hitting targets. Most young managers experience their first job as a relentless exercise in target hitting. Leadership is much more than hitting the bull's eye. There is a large human component in leadership behaviour. Young managers have to explore hitting deeper chords in human nature rather than just hitting targets.

Leadership is about mobilizing the energy of people towards the strategic goals and tactical targets. Moving people is vastly different from moving paper on a desk or a cursor on a computer screen. Moving people demands that you learn to decode human psychology of high performance. Leadership is about getting people to hit targets not when they are told to but when they are inspired to. This makes the difference between a mechanical and a magical performer.

In the world of crisis and uncertainty, the target is rarely a fixed one. Volatility in the business landscape creates moving targets. The priority of a leader is to enable target hitters to have a clear vision. They need clarity about which of the moving targets to hit and when. Take this example. In the post-COVID-19 world, most governments have struggled to balance the targets of safety and economy. During prolonged lockdowns, the target was to secure the health and well-being of citizens. This slowed down the performance of governments in achieving their economic targets. Most leaders struggled to balance these two competing targets. But there were a few leaders who navigated the dynamic challenge of choosing their targets well. Surprisingly, some women heads of states did steer their countries better than their male counterparts. One of them is New Zealand's young prime minister, Jacinda Ardern.

Under Ardern's leadership, New Zealand, which relies significantly on revenue generated by tourism, closed its borders to international travel on 19 March 2020. This was done only 19 days after the first confirmed COVID-19 case. It was one of the earliest and most stringent lockdown imposed. Ardern said, 'A strategy that sacrifices people in favour of, supposedly, a better economic outcome is a false dichotomy and has been shown to produce the worst of both worlds: loss of life and prolonged economic pain.'

Balancing pragmatism and idealism, Ardern represents the ethos of new leadership in our volatile, uncertain, chaotic and ambiguous world. Jacinda Ardern, commenting on her style of leadership, said, 'Very little of what I have done has been deliberate. It is intuitive. I think it is just the nature of an event like this. There is very little time to sit and think in those terms. You just do what feels right.'

Young managers will not have the luxury of problem-solving by elaborate meetings and threadbare analysis. They have to learn to fix a plane even while flying it. This will be the new normal in the post-COVID-19 world.

What does true leadership in a crisis look like? You only have to look at former British Vogue cover star Jacinda Ardern, the prime minister of New Zealand, who has taken a 20 per cent wage cut in line with her country's residents and has not only flattened the curve but squashed it too! Ardern, the youngest female head of government at the time of ascension, has led spectacularly by smashing several glass ceilings. Ardern, who already set an example of the challenges and competence of working mothers won people over with the way she led the country in the aftermath of the horrifying Christchurch mosque shootings. Within 36 hours of the shooting, she had mobilized politicians to tighten up gun laws, and less than a week later, she announced immediate changes banning assault rifles and military-style semi-automatics. She led the final bill reading with these emotional, impassioned words: 'They (victims) will carry disabilities for a lifetime, and that's before you consider the psychological impact. We are here for them. I could not fathom how weapons that could cause such destruction and large-scale death could be obtained legally in this country.' She has exhibited the same leadership attributes in the COVID-19 crisis: 'I refuse to believe that you cannot be both compassionate and strong,' she had said. Her tools were scientific approach (four-level COVID-19 alert system), clear communication (being credible by citing numbers and simple graphs to get her message about flattening the curve as well as her daily live stream messages of encouragement from her home, sometimes, even sitting on her bed!) and keeping compassion (understanding how the virus behaves, she said, 'We won't see the positive benefits of all of the effort you are about to put in for self-isolation … for at least 10 days. So don't be disheartened….') at the core of decision-making. By providing a type of leadership that combines strength, inclusivity and empathy, Ardern, prime minister of a tiny island nation, is an icon that most world leaders would want to learn from.

✳ 2 ✳

MANAGERS AND LEADERS

The world is changed by your example, not by your opinion.

—Paulo Coelho

MANAGERS HAVE POSITION; LEADERS HAVE DISPOSITION

Think of the emergency ward of a leading hospital. A patient with an acute respiratory problem is rolled into the ward by an attendant. It is a crisis situation. There is no time to lose. Everybody in the emergency ward is geared up to attend the patient. There are no command structures, no hierarchies here. The chief of administration, doorman, nurses, surgeon— everyone around the patient choreographs perfect team-work to make sure the patient receives a prompt and reliable medical care.

Compare this with a pedestrian wanting to get a first information report (FIR) registered in a police station, in India, for a roadside accident involving a drunken driver of a car. The pedestrian shuttles between one navel-gazing police officer and another. After three hours, the police station decides that the said accident actually happened in a place that was under the jurisdiction of another police station. By the time the accountability is fixed, the exasperated pedestrian decides not to lodge the FIR as he fears that he may be hauled up for doing a citizen's duty.

In the first instance, it is people driving an organizational structure to meet a goal. In the second instance, it is the structure preventing people from accomplishing a legitimate goal. The first is the example of a leadership-driven organization. The second is bureaucratic management at work. Professor John Kotter (1999) of the Harvard Business School, from whom I had learnt many lessons in leadership, makes an important point:

> A peacetime army can usually survive with good administration and management up and down the hierarchy, coupled with good leadership concentrated at the very top. A wartime army, however, needs competent leadership at all levels. No one yet has figured out how to *manage* people effectively into battle; they must be *led*.

Management is about the position; leadership is a disposition that goes beyond positions. Managers minimize risks; leaders maximize contribution. Managers work through structures of stability; leaders work through dynamic change. While managers are defined by their position, leaders can emerge from any position. All they need is the willingness to change the status quo and commit to action. Gandhi, the quintessential leader, once said, 'It's not just words. Action expresses priorities.' Gandhi held no significant position in his life. He was neither the head of a state nor was he commander of an army. Yet he led from wherever he found a rationale for changing the status quo. He led without a designation or title and accomplished the near-impossible task of gaining independence for his nation.

Mayo Clinic's chief administrative officer, Jeffery Bolton, was asked as to how does a small town of 125,000 people has the number one rated healthcare system in the world? His response to it was,

'Mayo Magic!' Founded more than a century ago by two brothers in the rural Midwest, Mayo Clinic is a non-profit health system that cares for more than a million people with difficult-to-treat conditions and focuses on the mantra 'patients first'. The health system fosters teamwork here, not hierarchy. It's like a bee that wants to make honey. You do not issue protocols on solar navigation or carbohydrate chemistry; instead, you put it together with other bees (and you'd do this quickly, for solitary bees do not stay alive) and you do what you can to arrange the general environment around the hive. So if one doctor is unsure about a patient's treatment, they are immediately referred and moved to the next expert depending on the problem and speciality. Thus, according to Mr Bolton, the system's philosophy has always been that 'wisdom of peers is greater than any individual.' Mayo Clinic is a physician-led organization. It follows the 'leadership dyad' model where the physician leader is paired with an administrative partner. Importantly, they don't just say they focus on integrated care, they do it. Everything is aligned in that direction.

Remember the difference between a boss and a leader: a boss says, 'Go!'—a leader says, 'Let's go!'

—E. M. Kelly

MANAGERS ARE DEDICATED TO TASKS; LEADERS ARE DEVOTED TO PEOPLE

Anil Manibhai Naik, group chairman of the engineering conglomerate Larsen & Toubro, aptly described the innate character of a leader:

> If the person has devotion, passion, conviction and commitment—half the job is done. For the rest of the capabilities, a person can be groomed. (Gopalakrishnan and Mody 2020)

Managers are dedicated to their positions and output. Leaders are devoted to purpose and outcomes. Naik then explains why leaders are rarer to find than managers, 'Not many have the devotion. Everybody does the hard work, but that is to maintain the job. If you are dedicated, you might add some value, but if you are devoted, you will multiply value.'

The difference between dedication and devotion is the difference between adding and multiplying value. Think of this story:

On 24 January 1848, James W. Marshall, a foreman found a bright shiny metal near a lumber mill. A carpenter, originally from New Jersey, Marshall found flakes of gold in the American River at the base of the Sierra Nevada Mountains near Coloma, California. When the news spread, people started rushing from all over the world to California to get gold. The gold rush lured people to abandon their homes and sell their belongings for a pot of money. Gold-mining towns grew like mushrooms all over the region, complete with shops, saloons, brothels and other businesses seeking to help determined and dedicated gold diggers. While everyone was running to get gold, a young man in one of those newly sprung up towns was busy crafting iron shovels with great devotion. When he was asked why he was not running to get some gold and devoting himself to making iron shovels, the young man responded, 'I am thinking of the hardships of these people running past me. When they try and dig for all the gold, they will need my strong shovels to do the digging. They will soon rush towards my workshop and buy those shovels for the price of gold.'

Dedication to a task makes you a factor of production. This is like digging for gold like everyone else does. Devotion to those people who will need the shovels makes one a factor of creation. Leaders multiply value, creating something new.

They use their ingenuity to make people more productive rather than just being part of the production process.

Devotion is not a mechanical chore but meaningful and heartful contribution to whatever one does. Haven't we heard the story of the three bricklayers doing the same task of breaking bricks? When asked, what he was doing, the first bricklayer said he was just laying bricks for a wage. The second one, when asked the same question, said that he was dedicated to the construction of a temple. The third one, facing the same question, replied, 'My work is a devotional service rendered to the people who would come to visit the Lord residing inside the temple.'

MANAGING BY CLOCK, LEADING BY COMPASS

Organizations have come a long way since Frederick Winslow Taylor taught us management by the clock. A US industrial engineer, Taylor published his book *Principles of Scientific Management* in 1911. He laid down the fundamental principles of large-scale manufacturing through assembly-line factories. He introduced time and motion study for optimum job performance, cost accounting, tool and workstation design. Taylor broke down a complex task into small, simple steps. He then observed the sequence of movements taken by the employee in performing those steps. He carefully observed to detect and eliminate redundant or wasteful motion. He then measured the precise time taken for each correct movement. From these time and motion studies, he determined production and delivery times and computed prices for a product and incentive schemes for employees.

Taylor's contribution to management known as Taylorism was a critical factor in the dramatic rise of US factory output.

This led to the victory of the Allied forces in the Second World War. Taylor's legacy was inherited by the US automobile pioneer Henry Ford. Taylor wanted to improve machine and worker efficiency. Ford used the same principle for minimization of costs instead of maximization of profit. Both Taylorism and Fordism were the philosophical foundations of managing by the clock.

However, with the rise of service industries and the advent of the information age, management by the clock was unable to capture non-linear and complex value creation in an enterprise. The output of a knowledge worker who works on flexitime and flexible space cannot be captured by time and motion study. Knowledge work is largely intangible, unlike the production of goods. The knowledge worker does not work eight hours a day per week inside a factory. In his radical book, the *4-Hour Workweek*, author Time Ferry argues that it is not only possible to accomplish more by doing less but also mandatory. Knowledge work is driven by the worker's unique strengths and passion. Knowledge work is self-directed and not supervisor-driven. The worker's internal compass propels knowledge work. It does not matter how long a knowledge worker stays in office. It matters how they create, capture and disseminate new knowledge. It matters how they transform new knowledge into organizational competencies. While production work is moving physical objects in physical space or on an assembly line, knowledge work is about transporting a mental configuration in digital space.

Careers are a jungle gym. Not a ladder.

—Sheryl Sandberg

The movement from the clock to the compass is the transition from management to leadership. The clock is still critical for routine work that can be robotized. The faster and the

 KARMA SUTRAS

more efficient the robot, the better managed is routine work. However, it requires a compass to define what is mission -critical work. A compass gives meaning and direction to intangible work. A leader can outsource the clock to a robot, but they have to insource the compass.

MANAGERS HAVE SUBORDINATES; LEADERS HAVE FOLLOWERS

Managers spend a lot of time in status checking. They want to establish their own co-ordinates in the organizational hierarchy: Who is the boss? Who is reporting to whom? What are the rules of the game? How do I get noticed? How do I get to my next promotion? Instead of focusing on significant goals, young managers get busy a lot of time in upholding their own significance. They get into competitive rivalry with their peers. They talk to their bosses in the language of constraints. There is nothing wrong in status management. It is just that it drains a lot of productive energy of the manager.

Leaders, on the other hand, are in the business of creating value rather than claiming valuable tags and titles. They create value by influencing people to excel and to be more productive than they were before. In the presence of a leader, people feel more energized and optimistic about themselves. Managers drive subordinates. Leaders discover followers. Followership is the informal relationship that grows between a leader and followers when a leader has something meaningful to offer to them. In the age of information, it is the follower that creates the leader.

If you look at today's social media, you will recognize that leaders from all walks of life have a follower fixation. Whether it is Twitter or Facebook, the reputation of a leader is established by the quantity and quality of their followers. The network of followers establishes the credentials and shapes the career of the leader. Facebook's chief operating officer (COO), Sheryl Sandberg (2013, 53), describes the career paths of contemporary leaders in a powerful sentence in her book *Lean In*:

> Careers are a jungle gym. Not a ladder.

That's how leaders grow in their careers. They take on unexpected challenges and co-evolve with their people. It is the energized and empowered followers that make a leader, not the other way around.

In the age of knowledge, no one follows a leader blindly. With the advent of 360-degree appraisals, inside major corporations, subordinates and peers review their bosses. Even in the hallowed portals of academic institutions, technology has flattened the pedestal on which teachers once stood. The sage on stage is now, at best, a guide by the side. A teacher's ability to control the flow of information top-down is declining by the day.

Leadership in the third decade of the 21st century will be built by inspired and well-informed followers. Like a natural leader, there would be natural followers. Leadership skills will not be about managerial pecking order, authority or control. The word 'leader' would be a code name for purpose, principle and possibility. They will be more invested in caring rather than competing. Leaders will not crave spotlight for themselves. They will rather make the journey luminous for many other followers. In simple words, leaders will look for leaders, not just followers!

Sheryl Sandberg, COO of Facebook, in her book *Lean In: Women, Work, and the Will to Lead* conveys that even with gender biases in the workplace, excuses and justifications won't get women anywhere.

KARMA SUTRAS

Instead, you must 'lean in', give it your all and never doubt your ability to juggle family and career any day, any time. She believes that this bias is at the very core of why women hold themselves back. When a woman excels at her job, both men and women will comment that she is accomplishing a lot but is 'not as well liked by her peers'. She is probably also 'too aggressive', 'not a team player', 'a bit political', 'can't be trusted' or is 'difficult'. She refers, early on, in the book to a study showing that for men, success and likability are positively correlated, whereas, for women, they are inversely correlated. She also tells to stop trying to have it all. 'When I remember that no one can do it all and identify my real priorities at home and at work, I feel better—and I am more productive in the office and probably a better mother as well. Instead of perfect, we should aim for sustainable and fulfilling,' says Sandberg. She writes about a 2002 survey of medical students in a surgery rotation showing that women gave themselves lower scores than the men even though faculty evaluations gave the women higher ratings. Sandberg underlines how tough it can be, as a woman, to accept praise. She says,

> The hard work of generations before us means that equality is within our reach. We can close the leadership gap now. Each individual's success can make success a little easier for the next. We can do this—for ourselves, for one another, for our daughters and for our sons. If we push hard now, this next wave can be the last wave. In the future there will be no female leaders. There will just be leaders. (Sandberg 2013, 172–173)

MANAGERS PERSONALIZE CONFLICT; LEADERS HARVEST CONFLICT

Imagine yourself rowing a boat on a placid lake during a spring evening. A gentle breeze is blowing across the lake and cooling the atmosphere around you. Suddenly, you experience the thud of a heavy object hitting your boat from behind. You are jolted. You turn around and see that another empty boat has drifted from the lakeshore and accidentally dashed against your boat. What do you do under the circumstances? You understand that it is the law of physics at work: Two boats cannot be at the same place and at the same time without colliding with each other. You then gently move the empty boat away from your path and row forward.

Now, imagine that instead of an empty boat there is a man sitting on the boat that just hit you. What would be your likely reaction? You will most likely get upset or angry at the man sitting there. You will personalize the collision as the negligence of that individual man. Isn't that so? This is what most managers do when they face a situation like this: They personalize conflict. Most managers end up dealing with the emotional tension and polarization caused by a conflict—me versus you, us versus them, finance versus HR.

One of my teachers in conflict resolution, George Kohlrieser, was a hostage negotiator for over 45 years. From his years of dealing with hostage situations, he realized that managers in conflict situations cannot often separate the person from the problem. It is as though the manager's mind is held hostage by the person who is seen as the root of the problem. Who messed up becomes more important to find than detecting what went wrong with the system. This leads the manager towards witch-hunting rather than going to the systemic causes behind the disagreements.

Leaders explore deeper dimensions in a conflicting situation. They understand the subtle undercurrents of human nature. Leaders make the distinction between a passing interest and a deeper need in a human situation. According to

George Kohlrieser, interest is often superficial, such as land, money or a job, whereas a need has deeper roots, such as identity, security and respect. Many conflicts appear to be about immediate interests, but in reality, the behaviour of the people involved is driven by needs. For example, a person who has lost a promotion may have had an apparent conflict with their HR manager for being denied promotion. However, a leader can detect that their deeper need is not the promotion but the emotion of isolation from their peer group. This helps the leader in dealing with the issue more sensitively.

Emotions arising out of conflict become fertile grounds for leaders for reinventing their world. Leaders harvest human creativity from conflict. Their vision channelizes this creative power of conflict towards rejuvenating people and re-energizing organizations. Think of the emotion of rage that Mahatma Gandhi had experienced being thrown out of the train because of the colour of his skin. On the night of 7 June 1893, Mohandas Karamchand Gandhi, a young lawyer then, was thrown off the train's first class, 'whites-only' compartment at Pietermaritzburg station in South Africa for refusing to give up his seat. He converted his anger into a revolution that was unprecedented in human history.

HOW DO YOU KNOW IF YOU ARE A MANAGER OR A LEADER?

Leaders and managers do not inhabit two different worlds. They do not come from Mars and Venus, respectively. They come from each other like an integrated and interdependent whole.

The word 'management' has been grossly devalued to mean 'manipulation' of people and processes. Similarly, leadership has come to mean power and status rather than service and

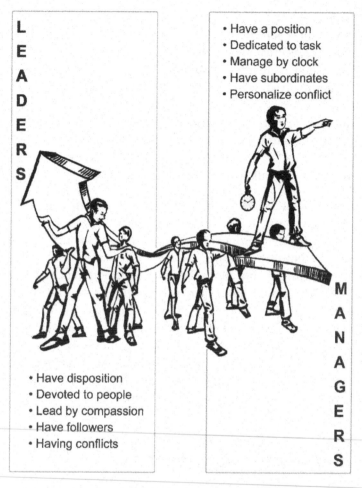

LEADERS

- Have a position
- Dedicated to task
- Manage by clock
- Have subordinates
- Personalize conflict

- Have disposition
- Devoted to people
- Lead by compassion
- Have followers
- Having conflicts

MANAGERS

contribution. These are sterile and static definitions. In the age of uncertainty, organizations need a dynamic interplay of both management and leadership. Organizations of the 21st century need the managerial attention to endless swarm of information as well as a leader's vision of the big picture. Think of a master chess player. If they aspire to be a grandmaster, they have to have both these core skills: visualization and computation. Visualization is the master's ability to create mental models of chess moves long before they actually appear on the board. This enables the grandmaster stay several steps ahead of their competition. At the same time, they have to have the computational skills with their eye on the chessboard and have to map the hard reality of their position with respect to their competition. If they have both, like the grandmaster in chess, they have integrated the best of the elements of management and leadership.

✻ 3 ✻

POWER AND AUTHORITY

Nearly all men can stand adversity, but if you want to test a man's character, give him power.

—Abraham Lincoln

POWER AND AUTHORITY ARE TWO DIFFERENT DIMENSIONS

Most young managers often confuse authority with power. In the organizational context, power is the capacity to do work and get work done. It is internal. It is something that grows from within you. Take the case of a management trainee who holds the attention of his senior managers in a meeting by the sheer clarity of his thought and the originality of his ideas. The trainee has little authority, but he is exercising his knowledge as power.

Authority, on the other hand, is external. It is what an organization or an institution gives you. Take the case of the same meeting where the young trainee demonstrates power. The authority to conduct the proceedings of the meeting, however, rests with his boss—the convening manager. He can shut the trainee down using his authority. The manager's authority is legitimized by the organization.

Whereas power is associated with human capacity, authority is associated with organizational structure and rules. Those with authority are not necessarily leaders. They are often unable to take risks and challenge the status quo, which are foundational elements in leadership. Most people in authority quote precedence and past practices. They can't mobilize their energy to lead as their feet are often stuck in procedural underwear.

In uncertain times, applying authority or institutionally sanctioned power becomes very challenging. People look to authority for providing order and equilibrium. In a very volatile world when equilibrium itself is threatened, it is difficult to hold onto an authoritarian position. Think of how the British colonial power was losing its authority when Mahatma Gandhi and the leaders of India's freedom movement challenged British rule.

Authority is about reinforcing structure and stability. Leadership, on the contrary, is about changing structure and challenging established authority. Deep change requires sustained and distributed power, greater than what can be sanctioned by a single authority. Take the case of Wikipedia challenging the authority of the venerable Encyclopaedia Britannica. Founded in 2001 by Jimmy Wales and Larry Sanger, Wikipedia was established to harness the collective knowledge of the world in the digital age. The founders put together a crowdsource and openly edited encyclopaedia. As the popularity of the website increased, people with dubious expertise began to post content on Wikipedia. The founders began to impose restrictions around unlimited access to posting with no checks as they would potentially bring into question the credibility of Wikipedia. This was necessary as an increased number of users began quoting Wikipedia as a trusted reference. The restrictions, while limiting access across the site, proved to be the right corrective step. In 2005, *Nature* published an article that studied 42 science articles in the Encyclopaedia Britannica versus in Wikipedia and found that the quality of the information in Wikipedia was comparable with that of the Encyclopaedia Britannica.

Wikipedia challenged the long-established authority of Encyclopaedia Britannica spanning more than two centuries. They changed the dominance of the multivolume Encyclopaedia that attempted to systematize human knowledge by expanding the power base of expertise that was digitally sourced from a larger number of experts.

While authority controls the base of power, leadership questions the power base and, ultimately, alters it. This is what Gandhi did when he started a mass movement that non-violently questioned the legitimacy of British authority. Gandhian leadership silently overturned the British Raj and brought freedom for India.

One of the most successful American executives of Indian origin, Indra Nooyi was a prominent female leader in the corporate sector whose story is both powerful and simple. Known for her unique leadership style in which she used to write reports to the parents of employees who perform exceedingly well, she is a living example of someone who can assume the role of a wife, mother and chief executive of a global conglomerate with dexterity. Ms Nooyi recalled a story about getting a call when she was at work late one night from the chairman and chief executive of PepsiCo that she was going to be named the president of the company and put on the board of directors. She left work to share the news with her family, but when she arrived home, she was met by her mother, who told her to go back out and buy milk for the morning. She did, banging the milk on the counter and telling her mother that she had just been named the president and placed on the board of a large company. Her mother simply said, 'You might be the president of PepsiCo. You might be on the board of directors. But when you enter this house, you're the wife, you're the daughter, you're the daughter-in-law, you're the mother. You're all of that. So leave that damned crown in the garage. And don't bring it in the house.'

Power in an organization is the capacity generated by relationships.

—**Margaret A. Wheatley**

YOU CAN HAVE POWER EVEN WITHOUT AUTHORITY

Can you be a leader without a suit, tie or trappings of formal authority?

Amul was formed as a part of a cooperative movement against Polson dairy in Anand, Gujarat, which procured milk from local farmers of Kaira district at very low rates and sold it to the then Bombay government. Everyone except the farmers benefited from this trade. The Gujarat Cooperative Milk Marketing Federation (GCMMF) was created in 1973 to market milk and all milk products produced by six district cooperative unions in Gujarat. GCMMF is the largest exporter of dairy products in India and Amul is the umbrella for all of its products. Over the last five and a half decades, dairy cooperatives in Gujarat have created an economic network that links more than 3.1 million village milk products with millions of consumers in India. GCMMF is a unique organization. It is a body owned by 12 million farmer members, managed by competent professionals serving a very competitive and challenging consumer market. As co-owners, the farmers have power over professionals who are hired to run the cooperative. It is a true testimony of synergistic national development through the practice of modern management methods.

It was possible for farmers to assume leadership once they came together sharing and co-owning resources in the co-operative federation. Leadership, sometimes, works in the opposite way that authority works. In order to change an exploitative system that denied farmers their due, Amul's leadership had to challenge the status quo and the authority of Polson dairy. Leaders, often, have to dismantle existing systems and create new ones, whereas authority is about preserving old structures and power equations. Traditionally marginalized groups such as farmers, who have never enjoyed formal authority in any organization, are able to exercise power in Amul. They hold power without a suit, tie or any high post.

We witnessed a shift in the balance of power between sellers and buyers of a product in the last 30 years. In the first two-thirds of the 20th century, large corporate houses were in charge of the marketplace. These companies had the authority to throw whatever they produced at customers. They also manipulated demand through big-budget advertisements. But that world has changed. In the electronics market, in Japan, a product barely survives for a few days as consumer preferences change. Today, customers have instant access to reliable information and have options; they can choose firms that delight them and avoid companies that do not deliver. The result is a fundamental shift in power in the marketplace from the seller to the buyer. Not only has the buyer the right to demand but also the right to be delighted by a product.

It is not power that corrupts, but fear. Fear of losing power corrupts those who wield it and fear of the scourge of power corrupts those who are subject to it.

—**Aung San Suu Kyi**

ME AND MISSION: ANATOMY OF POWER

Power is one of the deepest aspirations of a human being. A king seeks power over his kingdom, while a monk seeks power over his own senses. The capacity to use power is inborn. The anatomy of power covers a whole range from self-centredness (me) to purpose-centeredness (mission).

For a young manager, the first base of power is their own character: the sum total of their physical, attitudinal, mental and moral qualities that distinguishes them from other people. What the manager does consistently over a period of time gets recognized as their character. A character can be shaped through practice. For instance, if a manager wishes to be recognized as 'punctual', they have to appear in meetings, corporate events and social gatherings consistently, on time. A manager can take one good quality or virtue at a time and add that quality to the repertoire of their character traits.

The second kind of power comes from the quality of a manager's interpersonal relationship. An entry-level manager may be endowed with very little formal authority, but they can build a trustworthy relationship with a senior manager in the hierarchy. The senior manager then serves as an ally of the rookie manager in the echelons of power. The senior can sponsor the rookie for important assignment and speak favourably on their behalf to the top management. This gives the young manager power beyond their authority.

The first two kinds of power centre around the 'me' of the manager. The third kind of power comes from mission or purpose centeredness. Take the story of Nipun Mehta.

In the late 1990s, Nipun decided to become a software developer at Sun Microsystems, in the mid of the dot com boom. Very soon, he was disenchanted with the greed in his surrounding and went to a homeless shelter with three friends to give something with no strings attached. This was a transformational and life-changing moment for the young manager in his mid-20s. After creating a website for the homeless shelter, the joy of giving led him to start an organization called ServiceSpace, an incubator for gift-economy projects. Since then, Nipun and his organization have not only built thousands of websites for free, but they have also started several projects that developed into international movements like Karma Kitchen, a pop-up restaurant run by volunteers where the bill is always zero and people pay for their successors.

Power grows exponentially in a purpose-centred life. The nucleus of power is the young manager's passionate commitment to a path that they find fulfilling. This leads to self-learning and self-discipline. When what the manager does begins to touch the lives of many other people, the power of purpose is unleashed. Purpose opens the manager's heart to the other-centred universe. Service to others precedes preoccupation with the self. A surge of energy and power flows into the heart in selfless service. What was all about 'me' gradually blossoms into a mission. The mission is powerful because it gives meaning and direction to human action. It answers the question of 'why' rather than the 'what' and 'how' of doing something.

He who has great power should use it lightly.

—**Seneca**

USE AND ABUSE OF POWER

Power grows in a leader when it is associated with meaning. Some managers tend to confuse meaning with manipulation. They selectively spread rumours about their own power in the hierarchy. They are particularly skilled at manipulating their subordinates into believing that they are indeed powerful. One such manager, who had an office on the fifth floor of an office building, would routinely be called for discussions by the chief executive, whose office was on the sixth floor. The manager would vanish from his chair with the words, 'Boss called', and promptly take the elevator to the sixth floor. This went on for a few days. When these calls to meet the CEO became too frequent, his colleagues got a little suspicious. They spied on the manager as he left his chair that day, ostensibly, to 'meet the CEO'. Soon enough, they found out the trick that the manager was playing on all his colleagues. He would go up on the sixth floor and visit the washroom for 10 minutes and come down again without meeting the CEO. In fact, the CEO had not even called him. Needless to say, the manipulative manager lost not just his credibility but also all the power he was fictitiously accumulating.

When organizations are structured in rigid hierarchies of authority, abuse of power becomes inevitable. In such organizations, young managers often have no voice in decision-making and resource allocation. As Peter Senge in the foreword to my book explains, when a manager rises to the place of authority that exceeds his virtue, abuse of power is inevitable. This shows up in nepotism, sexual harassment, monopolistic behaviour, formation of cliques, coteries and power lobbies.

The young manager has to learn to carefully navigate the world of power and politics. Whenever there is a lopsided distribution of power, politics kicks in. A manager may not play politics, but they have to understand the nature of use and abuse of power in an organization. Instead of always looking at the top of the organizational hierarchy, young managers should look around and below to bond with their peers as well as

KARMA SUTRAS

subordinates. Friendly relationships laterally and down below go a long way in ensuring that the young manager will receive reciprocal support from their colleagues when the chips are down.

The legendary Konosuke Matsushita of the Panasonic brand in Japan allowed his employees to continue to work in one of his factories despite post-war depression and this company incurring losses. Fired by the faith Matsushita had in their abilities, his workers went out into the streets of Osaka and Tokyo to sell the products of the company. His workers, eventually, turned this company around because their leader had trusted them to do so. Matsushita then gave the company to them, as he had earlier promised. When asked what made the turnaround possible, Matsushita simply said, 'I just held up an umbrella when it was raining.'

When you shoot an arrow of truth, dip its point in honey.

—**Arab proverb**

SOFT POWER IN HARD TIMES

Joseph Nye, a former dean of Kennedy School of Government and distinguished Harvard professor, defined power as the ability to influence human behaviour in three distinct ways.

The first is by providing incentives and payments or carrots. The second by coercion and punishment or sticks. There is a third dimension of using the power of attraction that he defined as 'soft power'. It works best when it is used as complementary to the hard powers of rewards or punishments.

How does soft power work in organizations? John Chambers, the former CEO of Cisco, knew that compassion was more than the right thing to do; it also had a positive impact on his organization. He set up a system to ensure that he was informed, within 48 hours, of any employee, anywhere in the world, experiencing a severe loss or illness. Once notified, he would personally write a letter and extend his support to that person. In this way, he instilled a top-down appreciation of the value of care and compassion throughout the company.

Have you heard the sound of a butterfly landing on a hard rock? It is one of the most beautiful sights in nature and also a lesson in application of soft skills.

Business communication classes often assert the importance of eloquence over reticence, the triumph of speaking over listening and the dominance of words over silence. Yet in corporate boardroom meetings, the one who speaks the least is the most heard. Conversely, most board members seem to switch off mentally every time a motor mouth opens their mouth.

I once heard the chairman of India's largest business house speaking for just two and a half minutes in the annual meeting of two hours. Those two and a half minutes provided enough discussion points for the entire leadership team to air their views. In the wheeling-dealing of the business world, the truth is often veiled in jargons and management mumbo-jumbo.

In corporate as well as private communication, active listening and reflective silence are important tools of soft power. The parent who speaks the least before their adolescent kids seems to retain their respect more. Adolescents rebel against spoken words as a force of coercion and compulsion. Forced expressions lose their power to influence. A toned-down, parental voice nourishes parent–child communication.

KARMA SUTRAS

There is power in the unspoken word. In these hard times when we have become information addicts and slaves to the spoken word, periodic silence soothes the heart and frees the mind. If you look around nature, you will see enough evidence of soft power at work.

You have to watch a butterfly's feet soft landing on a delicate flower. It is the most exquisite symphony of silence.

In 2000, when Alexandra Scott, then four, set up her own lemonade stand, little did her parents think that they were witnessing the start of a campaign that would live on even after their daughter was gone. Alex Scott was diagnosed with neuroblastoma, a form of childhood cancer just a few days before her first birthday. When she was four years old, she decided that it was time for her to give back. She told her mother that she'd like to raise funds for helping other kids just like her and she wanted to do so by holding a lemonade stand. With the help of her brother, she raised $2,000 that year. This idea started a national movement that thrust her into national fame, including appearances on The Oprah Winfrey Show and The Today Show. After she passed away at the age of 8, her fundraising phenomenon continued to inspire many people to create their own lemonade stands. Her legacy continues till date through Alex's Lemonade Stand, a foundation that has raised more than a hundred million dollars for cancer research.

* 4 *

CULTURE AND TECHNOLOGY

We humans are an extremely important manifestation of the replication bomb, because it is through us—through our brains, our symbolic culture and our technology—that the explosion may proceed to the next stage and reverberate through deep space.

—**Richard Dawkins**

DECODING CULTURE

Think of the online store you will go to in order to buy a book as a gift for a friend. I will be surprised if the answer is not Amazon. You can think of a place in the world where you can find the best of authentic Ayurveda treatment. Many of you will probably think of Kerala, in the southwestern tip of India. If you need to buy a pair of best sports shoes at the lowest possible price, you may imagine buying it from Decathlon.

A power brand that draws the attention of a large number of consumers to itself is created by intangible culture. Organizational culture is a shared pattern of values, beliefs and behaviours. Culture shapes our thoughts and directs our emotions in a specific way within the organizational context. Amazon's culture has scripted speed and efficiency of online delivery of gifts. Kerala evokes the image of natural, relaxing and alternate healthcare in the form of Ayurveda. Decathlon culture ensures sale of sportswear at a great price-performance point. Culture is like a switchboard that controls the operations of an electric circuit. The design of the switchboard determines which way electricity will flow. The design of a corporate culture determines how the broad pattern of behaviour will flow within and outside an organization.

Nitza Hidalgo defines three levels of culture as concrete, behavioural and symbolic. They appear in organizations like the surface and deep structure of an iceberg. The surface structure consists of concrete and the visible aspect of organizational life such as communication, dress and office design. The deep

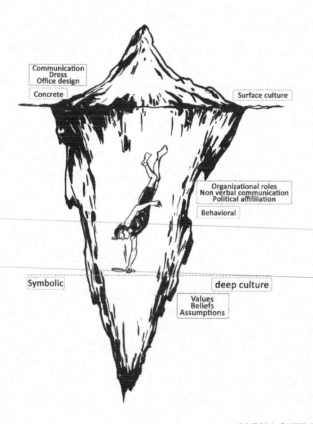

KARMA SUTRAS

structure consists of two aspects: behavioural and symbolic elements. Behavioural elements of organizational culture are organizational roles, non-verbal communication and political affiliation. The symbolic aspect of culture includes abstract elements such as values, beliefs and assumptions that the organization holds about the world.

A new entrant in an organization needs to decode both visible and invisible elements of culture.

Young managers entering an organization may have to look beyond the formal communication system to the subtler language of winks and nudges, through which the culture of an organization is communicated by its people. In a highly politicized organization, for instance, it is rare that a young manager is able to decode the actual meaning of messages and memos that routinely circulate in the organization.

HIERARCHY TO HYPERLINKS

Culture is formed on the basis of how people are connected to each other. Many organizations create cultures of extreme dependency, where subordinates have to depend on the seniors for resources. They have to respect those in the hierarchy based on seniority or number of years of service in the organization. Most people, in this kind of organization, are cautious about risk-taking as they look up to their bosses for critical decisions. Most government organizations function on dependent cultures. There is a second kind of organization where independent decision-making is encouraged and talented young experts are often promoted based on expertise rather than seniority. Many start-up organizations are examples of independent cultures. There is a third kind of organization where teamwork and collective leadership are nurtured. These are organizations like most IT, boutique consulting firms that work on the basis of interdependent leadership. Dependent, independent and interdependent cultures are evident in the way hierarchies are established.

In the new world of organizations, hyperlinks are replacing hierarchies. In this world, organization charts do not really work, and hierarchies are permeable. In the hyperlinked world, the young entrant or even a doorman can connect to the CEO or anyone outside the organization without having to seek layers of permission. Pyramids of ascending power structures are replaced by networks. Pyramids are buildings that grow bottom-up. Networks are like tress that can grow upward, downward or even sideways. Technology has pushed organizational intelligence from the limited hardware of the bosses' brain to software inside a computer, and now, everywhere through hyperlinks.

This is the age of knowledge work. However, the value of a knowledge worker is not derived from the amount of knowledge that they have stored in their heads. A knowledge worker may not have solutions to all the problems of the organization, but they have to have the information about where to find the solution. Knowledge organizations are not ossified fortresses of answers but laboratories to propagate the right questions. Centralized power structures of ascending hierarchies are outdated in hyperlinked organizations.

Think of the largest organization called the World Wide Web. The Web has no hierarchies, no central command and no management control. Yet even during a crisis situation like the post-COVID world, the Web functions seamlessly through hyperlinks. The speed of the internet is many times faster than the speed of chronological time. The Web connects us in space much faster than the COVID-19 virus. The speed and spread of the Web give us that extra edge over the virus that can make the difference between life and death.

KARMA SUTRAS

Young managers have to learn to deal with the crumbling of the sequential world of hierarchies. They have to wake up to the random universe of hyperlinks. Hyperlinked organizations are not comfortable with too much of management control. The power structure of pyramids based on fear does not hold good anymore. The new culture of hyperlinks is one of equity and equality. From the womb of the old organization, a new organization is emerging. The sooner leaders are able to decode this emergence of a new culture fuelled by technology, the better off they will be as leaders.

In its Bangalore campus of an Indian multinational technology company, the charismatic founder CEO wanted a culture change in his organization. He introduced the practice of wearing a formal tie for all employees one particular day, per week. Young managers, not attuned to the culture of formal wear in the office, wore those ties but removed them as soon as they were out of the sight of surveillance cameras. The CEO couldn't convince a whole generation of managers that a tie was only a visible surface of the invisible professional value of formality that he wanted to inculcate in youngsters. The company was founded in 1981 with just $250 and earned a revenue of $12.78 billion in 2020. Until 2001, meritocracy prevailed in the organization, resulting in its spectacular growth. After that, the company went too bureaucratic. The organization suffered as the founders imposed their own control over company culture and were unable to create leadership successors. The chief financial officer of the company left the organization saying, 'The founders have been dominating the management stream.' Restless junior managers have also begun to flood recruiters with their resumes. The company, once a dream organization for engineering and management graduates, had lost some of its past glory.

TECHNOLOGY SHAPES BEHAVIOUR AND CULTURE

How many times does an average manager switch on his/her smartphone in a day? Research says about 150 times. How does an innocuous pocket device end up shaping behaviour? It does so by making our minds addictive. Each time we open our phones to check for new notifications on LinkedIn or Facebook, the device blips a reward mechanism that works through our brain circuit. The more variable a reward, the more addicted we get to the process of groping for the reward. Most of social media gives us a menu of rewards in the form of likes, notifications or comments. These rewards appear intermittently in the form of blipping lights on our phones. The prospect of these periodic variable rewards makes our fingers itch to reach out for our smartphones.

Organizations of today work not in spans but spasms of attention. A computer now can detect the subtlest of expressions on our face such as tracking the movement of our eyeballs to be able to tell whether a customer looking at a particular product likes it or not. A hospital surgeon can analyse the chemical composition of a patient's breath to measure how they are feeling before surgery. A digital device in the doctor's hand can decode the proportion of chemical changes in the breath of the patient when their heart revs up and muscles become taut. In short, the patient's behaviour pattern reveals itself much before the patient expresses it in visible gestures.

Not just behaviour, technology is shaping the culture of organizations. It is shifting the balance of power from well-entrenched powers of an establishment to upstarts as well as start-ups. Social media is mobilizing popular opinion and political forces with lightning speed, as illustrated by the spread of the MeToo movement. Peer review sites allow garage-born enterprises to take on the most powerful multinationals. Key social media influencers can steer marketplace trends more impactfully than a global marketing campaign. A new culture shaped by technologies has unlocked vast new capacity to sense, connect, automate, amplify and augment human capability within organizations.

Tristan Harris, a former design ethicist at Google says that he is upset about technology hijacking the agency of a customer to make conscious and value-based choices while buying a product or service. 'We need our smartphones, notifications screens and web browsers to be exoskeletons for our minds and interpersonal relationships that put our values, not our impulses, first,' he says.

Despite the formidable success in connecting people, technologies are used as design tools to create a culture of interruptions around the world. Netflix and YouTube will auto-play the next episode of a video or a movie without allowing the viewer to make a conscious choice between playing and not playing the next episode. They, thus, interrupt the customer's ability to apply their own intellect in making the choice. This, of course, helps the business in promoting the habit of consumption. What it also creates is a culture of addiction to the sensory world.

TECHNOLOGY AND THE CULTURE OF FOLLOWERSHIP

Technology is applied knowledge. Over the years, from the bullock cart to the microchip, technology has amplified and extended the power of human beings. It has made life simpler for followers to engage leaders. Eldad A. Fux (2019), former chief technology officer and entrepreneur, says,

> I have always told my engineers that our job is not only to solve problems—that's the easy part. Our main job is to simplify problems. Simplifying a complicated problem helps us understand it better, and more importantly, to maintain it more easily and for a longer period of time.

From the time Johannes Gutenberg simplified the process of printing and distributing information in the 15th century, the power of the printed word moved from the central authority of priests and politicians to the masses of literate people. The internet has made transmission and access to information even more simple. With followers much better informed than ever before in the history of human civilization, a leader has to work much more diligently to earn the loyalty of followers. In order to connect with well-informed followers, leaders have to leverage the language of technology. Language is a system made up of symbols that allows a culture to be transmitted and shared widely. In high-tech environments, the language shifts within two to four years. Leaders have to ensure that they are aware and ahead of new trends and technologies.

The *New York Times* bestseller *The Decoded Company* describes how a company named Klick has made technology and culture inseparable. A Canadian digital agency specializing in healthcare, Klick has pioneered applying digital technology to (a) provide real-time coaching to enable talent and to automate processes, (b) use data as a sixth sense to inform decision-making and (c) create a talent-centric organization.

There is a culture of hyper-transparency, where an entire project team can comment on every aspect of their project. Performance feedback happens every week. And every transaction, interaction, input and outcome is stored in a 'wisdom layer' of data that enables 'gut feel' to be combined with data to inform rich insights. AI brings predictive insights to inform

KARMA SUTRAS

the company whether a contract will be profitable or a recruit will be successful.

Klick, an organization of 700 people, has just 5 people in finance, no HR department, no annual review process and remarkably few administrative assistants. It has sustained a consistent 40 per cent annual growth rate, high levels of profitability, less than three per cent voluntary attrition (in an industry where rates are typically near 20%) and public recognition for its contributions to a broader society. Klick leads by empowering and engaging people in a democratic way.

In the age of disruption, leadership is ultimately defined by its ability to sustain followership. As leadership becomes more democratized and distributed, more followers are able to find their voice in a collective enterprise. Followers are truly engaged with the work at hand when their voices and contributions are truly acknowledged.

TECHNOLOGISTS HAVE TO LEARN TO BE STORYTELLERS

Culture is invisible like the flow of electric current. Just as electricity is channelled through a switchboard, culture is transmitted through stories and myths that circulate within an organization. Stories are the switchboards of culture.

Technologists, by virtue of their profession, are not trained as storytellers. They develop language skills of functionaries. Most engineers place products before people. They talk of nuts and bolts of business. Yet what moves people in organizations are not nuts and bolts but aspiration. Gustave Eiffel was an engineer. He is best known for the Eiffel Tower he built for the 1889 Universal Exposition in Paris and his contribution to building the Statue of Liberty in New York. On 30 March 1885, while presenting a paper on the Eiffel Tower project,

Gustave Eiffel (Wikipedia 2020, 10 June) lifted his narrative beyond the technical problems and practical aspects of the tower to the story of aspiration of the people of France:

> Not only the art of the modern engineer, but also the century of Industry and Science in which we are living, and for which the way was prepared by the great scientific movement of the eighteenth century and by the Revolution of 1789, to which this monument will be built as an expression of France's gratitude.

J.R.D. Tata, the iconic leader of the Tata Group, was himself not an engineer. But he had recruited some of the best engineers to head his enterprises. One of his engineers, who later became a CEO, was explaining the intricacies of a newly purchased blast furnace in precise technical details in a Tata Steel plant in Jamshedpur. J.R.D. Tata held the engineer by the arm and asked, 'Have you thought of the poor worker who will operate the furnace at that extreme temperature? Have you thought of him as much as you thought of the furnace?' It was, perhaps, the storytelling capabilities of the Tatas that made Tata Steel advertise its aspiration as 'We Also Make Steel'. This signalled that human aspiration would always precede the product of the aspiration. Steelmaking is a by-product of that aspiration, just as a toy is a by-product of the imagination of the toymaker.

Why does a technologist need to turn data and information into a narrative? The world out there is super-saturated with information. Most technologists think that the world needs better information. Actually, the world waits to be *informed* better. Stories are the most powerful vehicles for informing people better. Intricate plots, the challenge of contexts, the trials and triumph of heroes inhabiting stories—these elements make for their memorability. Most importantly, stories, unlike dry data, are about people like you and me, in flesh and blood.

Nolan Bushnell, an American electrical engineer and the father of video gaming, is known for establishing Atari Inc. Nolan Bushnell famously said,

> These days when you say 'videogame', people think of immersive games that take over your life and require three thumbs to control. My goal is to create games that almost retreat into the background. I'm interested in bringing them back to their role as a social facilitator, the way party games help people to interact.[1]

Atari paved the way for young entrepreneurs like Steve Jobs and Bill Gates, and people who came after them, to venture into their enterprises. Here is how Bushnell told the story of his business to the larger world of aspiring young leaders, 'Business is a good game—lots of competition and a minimum of rules. You keep score with money.'

The pendulum of progress, be it slow or fast, is always in motion. Some companies rise to the top while some drop, some innovate and disrupt. Take, for example, Intel. Intel chips won in the PC world but started buckling under pressure in the world of mobile computing, Internet of Things, cloud and wireless technology. To top it all, microprocessor chip sales started turning down when phones suddenly became computers. Soon, Apple became the most valuable company and they started manufacturing MacBooks with their own chips (based on Advanced RISC Machines [ARM] technologies with much lower power processor, but a better business model; by licensing its design to other companies that could manufacture their own products), leaving Intel behind, wondering about their slip in the disruptive trend. The topic

---

[1] https://www.brainyquote.com/authors/nolan-bushnell-quotes (accessed on 6 July 2020).

'how and why Intel missed the mobile market' is still a bone of contention. At the Intel Capital Summit, 2019, CEO Bob Swan described Intel Capital's role as a combination of strategy, finance and culture as they invest $132 million in AI start-ups. He said, 'We view our portfolio companies as one of those ways culturally that we can stay extremely contemporary with those that are doing massive disruptive things out in the tech world.' Having led the digital revolution for the past 50 years, Intel now stands at the threshold of transitions towards AI-based technologies by learning more from collaborations rather than starting from scratch thus going heavy on disruption.

* 5 *

DECODING WORK

Men acquire a particular quality by constantly acting a particular way. You become a just man by performing just actions, temperate by performing temperate actions, and brave by performing brave actions.

—**Aristotle**

THREE RULES OF WORK

Albert Einstein gave us three rules of work. They are:

1. Out of clutter, find simplicity.
2. From discord, find harmony.
3. In the middle of difficulty lies opportunity.

The first rule means the recognition of a specific ideal towards which we wish to work. Sony works towards being a company that inspires and fulfils your curiosity. Sony created world-class technology and products that moved people to embrace them. Gandhi worked for the simple ideal of non-violence, and his life was dedicated to that single cause. Such was the power of that cause that it enabled one man to stand up against the might of the British empire. Our day-to-day work-lives are cluttered with a thousand competing priorities.

Einstein's second rule is: From discord, find harmony. This is an extension of the first rule. The first step towards the search for harmony is to find coherence within one's own self in the context of work. This means that my head and my heart must be together in the work that I do. The next step towards the search for harmony in work is synchronicity. This is the alignment of our spontaneous work with the demands of the environment. The Greek philosopher Aristotle said, 'Where your talents and the needs of the world cross, there lies your vocation.'

The third rule of Einstein is: In the middle of difficulty lies opportunity. If we clearly analyze the elements of any difficult situation, we will come to understand that the crux of the problem lies more in ourselves than in the external situation. A champion mountaineer will tell you that the greater difficulty lies not in the steep slope that they negotiate but in the fear in their own hearts. Someone involved in car racing is worried not so much about a difficult bend on the track as they are about their unsteady nerves.

DEEP WORK IN THE WORLD OF DISTRACTION

From the perspective of leadership, there is much more to work than just getting a job. In fact, a significant percentage of those jobs that existed even five years ago would not exist in the next five years. On 20 June 2014, the first 3D-printed metal part, a humble titanium bracket, took to the skies on board a commercial jetliner. With this, aviation history was made by Airbus. Imagine how many design and manufacturing jobs a 3D-printed model aircraft will displace going forward! Not just manufacturing jobs, service sector jobs in legal, medical and other professions will yield ground to digitization and automation. In fact, all jobs that can be broken up into a simple cause–effect relationship will be taken over from a human being by a more efficient device.

A leader's work, fortunately, is deeper than what is demanded by a stereotypical job. Cal Newport's book raises this issue of deep work as the core of a leader's contribution in the age of automation.

> To remain valuable in our economy, therefore, you must master the art of quickly learning complicated things. This task requires deep work. If you don't cultivate this ability, you're likely to fall behind as technology advances. (Newport 2016, 13)

Deep work is the ability to focus on a chunk of a job for a sustained length of time without any distraction. If you are able to lend your entire attention to solving a problem in your organization for one hour of uninterrupted time, you will develop the ability to plug into a space of deep attention in your neural structure. This kind of work is difficult to replicate in the machine world. Newport explains further:

> The Deep Work Hypothesis: The ability to perform deep work is becoming increasingly rare and at the exact same time it is becoming increasingly valuable in our economy. ...the few who cultivate this skill, and then make it the core of their working life, will thrive. (Newport 2016, 14)

Decoding the history of people who have produced world-class work such as the biologist Charles Darwin or the author Charles Dickens, researchers have found that they never worked for more than four or five hours a day. However, their work was deep and uninterrupted by the onslaught of modern technology.

Someone aspiring to be a leader will need to set aside specific time to engage in deep work. They have to clear up digital-free time and stay away from smart devices that fragment attention. This will help them not only in doing high-quality work but also more efficient work. In short, deep work will help leaders produce better work in less time.

MODERN MISCONCEPTIONS ABOUT WORK

If you were to visualize your world as a limitless field of action, which it is indeed, your work would seem like a narrow, artificial boundary created by you. When you finish a job successfully and exclaim, 'I have done a great job today,' do you realize that your claim to greatness does not acknowledge the role of many other people who have contributed to your triumph? Do you acknowledge, for example, the following contributors to your success: the employer who gave you your job, your college teacher who taught you the skills necessary for it, your mother who brought you into this world, your father who paid your way through school, the compassionate colleague who helped you when you were in distress, the old farmer in South America who produced the breakfast cereal you ate in the morning and the orange tree in Florida whose fruit nourished you? If you did not acknowledge the role of all these people and many more besides, perhaps your statement, 'I have done a great job', would be only partially true. Our work is an expression of a universal field of action, yet we create an artificial definition (i.e., making something finite) out of an infinite dimension of our work. From this crisis of vision arises the following misconceptions about our work:

Misconception 1: Our work is equivalent to our qualifications.

Misconception 2: Our work is a 9-to-5 affair.

Misconception 3: Our work is a product, not a process.

MISCONCEPTION 1: OUR WORK IS EQUIVALENT TO OUR QUALIFICATIONS

In many of my workshops, participants introduce themselves as 'I am an engineer', 'I am an accountant', 'I am an ENT specialist' or some such qualification. To explore the element of truth implicit in the statement, 'I am an engineer', one may ask the following: 'Am I an engineer, or do I have an engineering qualification? Obviously, my identity as a human being in this world and society is much larger than an engineering degree.' One of the maladies of a highly specialized society is that our world view is often shaped and dominated by our skills at work. Sometimes, our world view shrinks so much that we begin to see ourselves as impersonal cogs in an economic engine.

MISCONCEPTION 2: OUR WORK IS A 9-TO-5 AFFAIR

A great illusion that we love to hold on to is that our work lasts only from 9 AM to 5 PM, after which we go home. The truth is that our entire existence is nothing but work. The very fact of our being alive is ample testimony that we are at work, whether we are breathing in or breathing out, working our muscles or exercising our minds, working for ourselves or in spite of ourselves. Taking into account the amount of work that nature does to keep us going (e.g., maintaining our heartbeats) should convince us that our work is not temporal but existential.

MISCONCEPTION 3: OUR WORK IS A PRODUCT, NOT A PROCESS

Often, what we do is perceived, defined and measured in terms of a product that is external to our efforts. Yet all significant work is really an intrinsic process of the unfolding of human consciousness. Even the most tangible product of our work is really a process. The men who invented the first hot-air balloon must have hailed their creation as evidence of humanity's final triumph over gravity. Had they lived to see the development of the most sophisticated rocket, they would have readily admitted that their balloon was only a small and visible step in an unending and invisible process of mankind's inner quest for perfection. Neil Armstrong, the first human to set foot on the moon (20 July 1969) said, 'That's one small step for man; one giant leap for mankind.'

So it is with all our work. We become caught up in the product or in the 'idea' of the product so much so that the process remains obscure to our limited vision. The glib, oft-heard expression 'mind over matter' exposes the limitation of a vision that sees the conquest of external nature by the mind as the only worthwhile work in this world.

LEADERSHIP = PLUMBING + POETRY

James March, one of my teachers, defines leadership like no one else has. Even if you are not a plumber or a poet, you will get the picture. Leadership is a hard science as well as silken art. Plumbing may sound boring yet is very essential and life giving. Think of the water that the plumber digs out with all the hard work. Water is the universal solvent. It dissolves even hard, rock-like problems. Good leaders, like plumbers, dissolve problems by digging deep. The hiss and hum of water that runs through a water pipe is the raw energy that leaders harness. A leader needs to dig deep into the hearts and minds of the followers. In this way, leaders can mobilize human energy. The flow of energy builds momentum that can solve and dissolve very critical problems. Good plumbing ensures fluidity that harmonizes a group of people into a high-performance team.

Plumbing demands efficiency and good judgement. It is the nuts and bolts of leadership action. It deals with the mundane and the methodical. You follow established procedures. Leaders who are plumbers have to take initiative, allocate resources, manage time and coordinate multiple activities. While plumbing is the science of leadership, poetry is the art of leadership. Poetry draws on insight, inspiration and imagination. Poetry kisses the soul of followers. It gives meaning to mundane tasks. The leader, as a poet, connects with other people. They communicate their passion through words. Leadership is like a performing art through which the leader gains entry into the subjective world of the follower.

Great leaders like Gandhi can convert the hard struggle of civil disobedience against the mighty British Empire in the language of heart-rending poetry: 'They may torture my body, break my bones, and even kill me. Then they will have my dead body, but not my obedience.'

Or think of Winston Churchill's first speech as Britain's prime minister. Churchill put in poetic form one of history's best battle cries against the Nazis:

> You ask, what is our policy? I can say: It is to wage war, by sea, land and air, with all our might and with all the strength that God can give us; to wage war against a monstrous tyranny, never surpassed in the dark, lamentable catalogue of human crime. That is our policy. (Churchill 1940)

Or think of the American President John F. Kennedy's inaugural address in 1961, when he inspires his countrymen to embrace national service—'My fellow Americans: ask not what your country can do for you—ask what you can do for your country.'

Through poetry, a leader breathes life and meaning into what would otherwise be difficult work. Poetry makes a dull task look unimaginably beautiful.

Leaders idealize the real through poetry and then realize the ideal through plumbing. Reality has both subjective and objective sides. Leaders have to learn to play in between these two fields like balancing on a see-saw. If a leader is too objective, they cannot evoke passion in their followers. If they are too subjective, their words will seem hollow and not backed by the concreteness of objective goals.

A nation that looks down upon good plumbing as a lowly activity and tolerates bad poetry because it is a pastime will have neither good plumbing nor a great vision; neither its pipes nor its principles will hold water.

Ever since COVID-19 swept the globe, the traditional office space has been put to rest and working from home is now the new norm. The style of work consisting of office spaces and cubicles is not a long-standing phenomenon, and even before COVID-19, it was already on its way out. A total of 80 per cent of US workers reported that they would turn a job down if it didn't offer flexible working arrangements. This lack of job flexibility has also impacted in a delay of starting a family for the sake of reaching a certain career level they felt comfortable with. This employee demand pushed remote work to grow 44 per cent since 2015. For this reason, COVID-19 has, really, only expedited what was already on the horizon. About the future of work, one thing is certain: Remote work is here to stay. This transition has already been set in motion with tech companies like Facebook taking initiative now by telling staff to work remotely for the remainder of the year and, in some instances, permanently. Google has begun to rotate employees on site for a few days each week while ensuring facilities remain at only 10 per cent occupancy. Twitter has taken a somewhat different approach where, virtually, all employees will work from home, permanently. The other shifts that come along with remote work include incorporation of AI into work and daily lives, promotions and merit rises becoming data-centric, methods of feedback (in office spaces, managers could quickly stop by their employee's desk and thank them for their efforts on a project but with remote work, instant messaging or a monthly video call to review projects must be undertaken to boost employee morale.), cybersecurity measures, etc., to name a few.

Part 2
SUTRAS

✳ 6 ✳

PERSONAL MASTERY

Your visions will become clear only when you can look into your own heart. Who looks outside, dreams; who looks inside, awakes.

—Carl Jung

THE ART OF SEEING

Personal mastery is a function of the quality of seeing. Most of us would look at a falling apple and soon forget about it, but it takes the insight of an Isaac Newton to see beyond the event and discover the force of gravity. We all see suffering around us. Yet it takes the insight of a Buddha to go to the root cause of human suffering and identify it as desire. Seers, as we call them, are found in all walks of life—business, sports, science and organized religion. To see is also to know and understand with clarity. In the middle of a counselling meeting with a non-performing employee, a team leader stops briefly and says to the employee, 'Oh, now I see your point.' In this 'seeing', the leader begins truly to understand the follower. Leaders are not content with facts. They have immense energy to discover newer versions of the truth. You may take a photograph of the ocean and give us facts about it. But can such facts encompass the whole truth of the ocean?

THE PLAY OF ENERGY

Every action, gesture, thought, intention, emotion and even the faintest flicker of our consciousness is a constant play of energy. When we look at the source of this energy from the point of view of raw materialism, we find that the same molecule of sugar that released the energy for Einstein's conceptualization of the theory of relativity is also responsible for Buddha's realization of nirvana as well as for Hitler's aggression against the world. Yet we know that merely studying the structure of a sugar molecule will not yield to us the secrets of an Einstein, a Buddha or a Hitler. Personal mastery comes not from merely accumulating energy but through processing this energy in the light of our awareness. Personal mastery is the science and the art of channelling energy from what we consider purposeless to that which we hold as purposeful. The Sanskrit word for energy work is *tapas*. The Japanese have a similar word, *shugyo*. Both *tapas* and *shugyo* mean the discipline of self-mastery. This means being aware of the nature of our energy body. It is the first step towards what the ancients called self-knowledge. Many of us fritter away our energies wallowing in negative emotions. We become irritable. We are gripped by anger or anxiety, which causes our muscles to tense up. All of these negative emotions eat away at our vitality and energy. I have often observed people contort their faces and frown during brainstorming sessions. My knowledge of human anatomy tells me that our brains do not have muscles. Yet how much of our energy do we unnecessarily lock into our facial muscles as we 'storm our brains'?

FROM CAPABILITY TO COPABILITY

Personal mastery is a function of both capability and 'copability'. When one's self acts on the environment, we demonstrate our capability. When our environment acts on one's self, what is tested is our 'copability' (ability to cope).

Our capabilities are measured in terms of our skills in negotiating the outward environment. Capability is the visible, tangible aspect of our competence. It is the outbound energy that shows up as our work, achievements, credentials, qualifications and all that we have done to carve out a niche for ourselves in the environment. In contrast, 'copability' is the energy that the self gathers together to face an unpredictable environment. The mechanism of 'copability' enables the body to shoot out adrenaline when we face danger or an enemy. The way in which we choose to deal with pain, loss and suffering also demonstrates our 'copability'. A man who is unable to get along with his wife becomes an alcoholic. An executive on the fast track misses a promotion and exhibits her sense of loss in the form of an ulcer. When the environment behaves in a manner that seems unpredictable to us, we find it difficult to cope. We fail to realize, however, that the environment 'out there' is merely our interpretation of it. To a great extent, our 'copability' depends on the way in which we interpret the reality of our environment. Pain and loss are apparent blocks that our environment places before us. We can interpret these blocks as obstacles to our happiness or as great challenges that we must overcome to receive even greater rewards. How then do we enhance our ability to cope? The only way we can do this is by enriching our perspective on what we may, at first, interpret as 'pain' or a 'lost opportunity' or a 'problem'.

FROM SELF-IMAGE TO THE REAL SELF

Many of our problems are self-created. The source of self-created problems is the fact that we mistake the self-image for our real self. Self-image is nothing but the accumulated projections of our identity. It makes us vulnerable to changes outside us. If our self-image is one of an evergreen youth, the appearance of the first grey hair makes us lose sleep. We are traumatized by a single rejection slip from an editor if our self-image is that of a successful writer. How does one go beyond the veil of self-image in search of the real self?

The quest for the self can begin only when we have turned our attention from the world outside to the world inside. This is also a transformation in the quality of our seeing: from mere sight to insight. The journey towards self-realization involves the disciplines of silence and solitude. Silence frees us from the noise of our exteriorized consciousness and allows us to probe our inner voice. Solitude enables us to be intimate with ourselves. I have often asked professionals from all walks of life, 'Who are you?' I receive predictable answers such as, 'I am an engineer, or a marketing manager, or an ENT specialist.' The next question I ask is, 'Who knows you are all of these?' This time, the answers revolve around 'mind' or 'thought'. Then I proceed to ask the final clinching question, 'Who knows you have a mind?' This time, a silence descends on my audience. In that silence, we begin to glimpse the truth of ourselves, which is that silence beyond all names and forms.

THE BODY: FOUNDATION OF THE SELF

We can begin to experience the notion of personal mastery in relation to our bodies by paying attention to the following:

1. One's environment does not lie outside one's body. Our bodies are part of what we understand as our environment. Sometimes what we think of as a problem 'out there' would not exist if we did not recognize it as a problem 'in here'. When we are physically unwell, even a bright day can look gloomy.

2. There is no real opposition between our inner and outer realities. The body is merely an intermediary between our inner and outer environments. When a body is fragmented, the entire universe appears fragmented. When a body is whole, the universe appears whole.

3. We are accustomed by the force of habit to pay attention to the world outside our bodies. Rarely does

our awareness dwell inside. We can cultivate the habit of looking within our bodies by interiorizing our consciousness.

4. One's body is a vast energy field that operates at several layers. These layers manifest themselves from the subtle to the gross. Each layer of energy corresponds to a certain level of awareness. By merely shifting our awareness, we can bring about profound changes in our bodies. Through awareness, we can heal ourselves and solve complex psychosomatic (body–mind) problems.

5. The energy of our being (awareness) is more subtle than the energy of our thinking. The energy of our thinking is more subtle than the energy of our doing.

6. When one's body is able to integrate several layers of energy into one unity, there is a breakthrough in awareness. When the energy layers in the body are fragmented, there is a breakdown in awareness.

7. A disintegrated body experiences chaos, disease and sickness. An integrated body experiences cosmos, ease and health.

Organizational learning based purely on abstract ideas is unlikely to help us solve real-life problems. The participation of the body in problem-solving is, sometimes, as important as the mind's engagement with the context of the problem. The following story illustrates this:

A philosopher, proud of his knowledge, hired an illiterate boatman to ferry him across a wide river in spate. While crossing the turbulent river, the philosopher, unable to restrain his tongue, constantly lectured to the boatman about the nature of existence. He asked the boatman several complicated questions about life. All the while, the boatman remained silent.

'Have you ever studied hydrodynamics?' asked the philosopher.

'No,' said the boatman.

'In that case, half your life has been wasted.'

The boatman said nothing.

Soon, a terrible storm blew up. The boat was tossed about by the wind. The boatman leaned towards the philosopher.

'Have you ever learned to swim?' asked the boatman.

'No,' said the philosopher.

'In that case, sir, all your life is lost, because the boat is sinking.'

THE SENSES: TAMING WILD HORSES

The *Katha Upanishad*, one of India's classical works of wisdom, describes the nature of our senses through the metaphor of horses pulling a chariot. The Upanishad says:

> *Know the body as the chariot itself.*
> *Know that reason is the charioteer,*
> *and the mind indeed is the reins.*
> *The horses, they say, are the senses,*
> *and their paths are the objects of sense.*

(Katha Upanishad, Verse 1.3.3)

The verse continues and we obtain a vivid picture of the discipline of personal mastery, which is compared to the taming of wild horses:

> *He who has not right understanding and whose mind is never steady is not the ruler of his life, like a bad driver with wild horses.*
> *But he who has right understanding and whose mind is ever steady is the ruler of his life, like a good driver with well-trained horses.* (Katha Upanishad, Verse 1.3.3)

KARMA SUTRAS

All classical wisdom has emphasized the discipline of the senses as an important step towards personal mastery. This discipline involves understanding the nature of the senses and acting on that understanding.

Leadership requires a quality that is often called 'common sense'. We cannot quite define what common sense is, yet we 'sense' it when we see it. Common sense comes from a freshness of perspective. Those with common sense not only ask the correct questions but also question the very premise on which these questions are based. Edward Deming, the pioneer of the total quality movement in industrial organizations worldwide, revolutionized management thinking through sheer common sense. Albert Einstein, who retained a child's innocence and inquisitiveness until the last day of his life, once said, 'Small is the number of them that see with their own eyes and feel with their own hearts.'

Great leaders have an unfailing grasp of the nature of reality. Buddha is, perhaps, one of those leaders who achieved a rare sense of proportion in his life. He discovered the middle path of right perception between austerity and indulgence and, consequently, led the world. Leaders lose their extreme follo-wing when they lose their hold on reality. George Bush, at the crest of a popularity wave after the First Gulf War, lost the US presidential election because he had not sensed the reality of the economic difficulties faced by his country and its people. Indira Gandhi, India's prime minister for two decades, suf-fered a disastrous loss in a general election because she failed to sense popular resentment against her policies.

The significant problems we face cannot be solved at the same level of thinking we were at when we created them.

—**Albert Einstein**

THE MIND: INNER INSTRUMENT

Try this experiment. Close your eyes for 30 seconds and visualize the word 'tree'. Observe any tree that appears on your mind's screen. Examine your mental picture down to the smallest detail. What do you see? A fir, maple or eucalyptus? A palm tree swaying in the breeze? Or did you see no tree at all? Did you see only the word tree written on your mental map? Perhaps, you saw the green leaves of the branches spreading like arteries. Perhaps, you saw the tree trunk or some flowers. Now ask yourself this important question: 'Did I visualize the roots when thinking of a tree?' Ninety-nine people out of a hundred will say, 'No.' But the roots, though invisible to you, do exist. Don't they? Indeed, the roots are the most important component of a tree. Yet why does our mind miss such an important portion of the tree while visualizing it?

Many specialists fail to solve the problems they themselves cause because their thinking becomes frozen and paralyzed in a given context. When a plan in an organization fails because of too much planning, which in turn stifles action, the planning department hardly notices it. Instead, it engages in even more rigorous planning without consulting the implementers, for instance, the managers in the field who may be able to pinpoint the flaws in the planning system.

The mind has been described in classical Indian wisdom as *antah karan*, the inner instrument. The instrumentality of the mind has not been confined to thoughts alone. In most Eastern civilizations, 'mind' and 'thought' are not synonymous. In these civilizations, the culture of the mind include the culture of both intellect and emotion.

The classical psychology of India identifies four states of the mind. The first state is when the mind is agitated (*kshipta*). In this state, the mind is in an emotional turmoil and cannot function to the fullest extent. For example, when we are angry or hurt, it becomes difficult for us to even answer a telephone call. The second state of the mind is when the mind is scattered (*vikshipta*). In this state, the mind is fragmented and distracted in different directions, as when we are trying to read a report, drink a cup of tea and answer a telephone call all at the same time. Needless to say, the mind cannot function with full efficiency in this state. The third state of the mind is the state of one-pointedness (*ekagra*). In this state, the energy of the mind begins to focus on a single object or idea. When we do something we love, the mind automatically becomes one-pointed. However, through constant practice, we can discipline the mind to be concentrated on anything that we choose. A concentrated mind is much more effective than an agitated or scattered mind. The ancient seers did not stop at a concentrated mind. They explored further and arrived at a state in which the instrument called the mind dissolved into pure awareness (*niruddha*). This is a state of transcendence in which one begins to have an intuitive grasp of reality.

As great leaders throughout history have often testified, emotion rather than intellect plays the primary role in decision-making. Mahatma Gandhi knew as he put it that, ultimately, one is guided not by the intellect but by the heart. The heart accepts a conclusion for which the intellect subsequently finds reasoning. Argument follows conviction. 'Man often finds reason,' Gandhi said, 'in support of whatever he does or wants to do.' Bertrand Russell echoed the same truth when he said, 'Even more important than knowledge is the life of emotion.'

THOUGHT IS NOTHING BUT A TOOL OF CONSCIOUSNESS

A thought is a tool of the human mind. It is a tool of our consciousness. If you are conscious of your thoughts, you can use those well. If you are not conscious, thoughts tend to use you indiscriminately. The process is similar to using a smartphone. If you know how to use a smartphone, it serves as a great tool. If you cannot handle a smartphone properly, it makes a fool out of you such as:

1. Sending misspelt messages such as 'your telephone operator embraced me' when the right spelling should have been 'embarrassed' me.
2. Making unintended calls such as the one to your most valued client at 3 AM in the morning.
3. Assorted acts of omission and commission including mistakenly sending a message to your boss that was meant to be sent to your pathologist.

You recognize that artificial intelligence goes hand in hand with natural foolishness. Coming from an unconscious state, you can see that your thoughts are often very illogical and have no apparent connection with each other. You can think of a toothbrush, and your thoughts may take you to the moustache of Hitler. From Hitler, your thoughts may wander around the Berlin Wall, the Great Wall of China and then to Wall Street in New York before you start thinking of a wall clock that you are afraid might fall on your head one day. From the toothbrush to a wall clock is a long-winding journey. We often lose ourselves in such mindless chatter.

SWITCHING THOUGHTS ON AND OFF

The way to a clear and decisive mind is to discover a thought-free conscious state that exists prior thoughts. Imagine a blackboard with nothing written on it. This analogy can be used to describe consciousness without the clutter of content. This consciousness is the pure potentiality of a human being. You can actualize this pure potential in as many ways as a smartphone can deliver applications. How do we get to clutter free consciousness? The only way to do this is by reducing the number of thoughts you think per minute (TPM). There are many methods of accomplishing this: You can simply practise being a conscious observer of your thoughts. If you find this exercise too abstract or difficult, you may simply focus your gaze on a burning candle or a sunset for five minutes without allowing too may intrusive thoughts. When TPM reduces in your consciousness, you begin to glimpse the silent witness that is you.

I prefer to surround myself with people who reveal their imperfection, rather than people who fake their perfection.

—Charles F. Glassman

TOWARDS AN INTEGRAL PERSON: THE LEADERSHIP EVOLUTION

Personal mastery is the ability to differentiate what we desire from what is desirable for us. This discipline not only enables us to make an intellectual distinction between the two but also empowers us to act on that distinction. All great leaders, all stable organizations and all enduring civilizations have made this crucial choice in the course of their development.

Leadership is not an outcome of a balanced personality but the evolution of an integral person. Etymologically, the word 'personality' comes from 'persona', which means a 'mask'. In the usual sense, this is what we understand by personality. It is a set of conventional social masks and an assortment of occupational skills that we use as a yardstick to measure a person's worth. But leaders wearing masks cannot inspire themselves or others. The true leadership profile is that of an integral person. Integral persons are those who integrate the energy of their thoughts and emotions with their work. Leadership comes naturally to integral persons for they serve with love. Their power of love is greater than the love of power.

An integral being experiences spiritual affinity with the natural order of the universe; their inner nature becomes one with outer nature. Their life becomes one song—a universe—of thought, feeling and action. Integrity is another name for this one song. It is a spontaneous expression of consciousness; it is not a conditioned behaviour. In this consciousness, our many aspirations are seen in their unity. We return to this unity at the end of our life's journey. True leadership, as we shall see in the next chapter, is a journey towards this integral consciousness.

* 7 *

CONSCIOUSNESS

The key to growth is the introduction of higher dimensions of consciousness into our awareness.

—Lao Tzu

THE NATURE OF CONSCIOUSNESS

The following story tells us a great deal about the nature of human consciousness. The hero of the story is Alexander, the great Macedonian emperor.

Alexander was camping on the border of the Indian subcontinent. He had marched triumphantly over half the world, conquering and subjugating one kingdom after another in fierce battles. In a sense, he was like the CEO of a multinational corporation battling local competitors and grabbing market share. In some places, he struck strategic alliances with local chieftains and held control. In other countries, he confronted his adversaries and raided their territories.

On the threshold of his passage to India, however, Alexander encountered a strange man. This man, dressed in a loincloth, would meditate for hours in a secluded place near Alexander's camp. For several days, Alexander saw this sage seated in a lotus position while looking towards the horizon. To Alexander, this sage seemed like a lazy man, a recluse who had dropped out of life's race. One day, the great warrior, unable to contain his curiosity, approached the sage and asked, 'Don't you have anything to do besides sitting and dreaming?'

The sage sat there unmoved.

'I see you every morning, evening and afternoon in the same place. You have not moved an inch. You must be a terrible fellow!'

The sage did not speak a word.

'Tell me, what is your goal in life?' demanded Alexander, exasperated.

Now, the sage smiled a little and said, 'Great warrior, you must first tell me about your goal in life before I tell you mine.'

Outraged, Alexander thundered, 'Don't you know I am Alexander? I am out to conquer the world.'

'What do you want to do after you have conquered the world?' the sage asked.

'I will then possess all the gold and all the elephants and horses in the world,' said Alexander, his lips curling in disdain.

'And then?' the sage asked.

'Then I will have all men as my slaves.'

'And then?'

'Then I will have all the women to serve me.'

'And then?'

'Then I will sit on my throne, relax and enjoy myself.'

The sage smiled. 'Sir, that is precisely what I am doing right now,' he said. 'Why are you bothering me? Please leave me alone and go ahead with your conquests.'

Both Alexander and the sage are leaders who envision their world in the light of their own consciousness. Alexander seeks fulfilment in the conquest of the outward world of form and phenomenon. The sage searches for peace in the inner domain of subjective experience.

Alexander's consciousness experiences the world as a battlefield, whereas the sage's consciousness experiences the same world as the field of self-realization. Alexander thinks, 'How much more do I need to be happy?' while the sage ponders, 'How much less can I have and still be happy?' Human motivation is in constant oscillation between these two questions that ring in our consciousness: 'How much more do I need to be happy?' and 'How much less can I have and still be happy?' The sage and Alexander live within all of us. They represent the two fundamental states of human consciousness.

THE EVOLUTION OF CONSCIOUSNESS

The very process of human development is an unfolding of the consciousness that permeates all life forms on this earth. Interestingly, the word 'development' has the same root as the word 'envelope'. Development simply means de-enveloping or opening up the scripts of our lives. Our mind–body–senses structure is like an envelope that acts as a cover for our consciousness. This consciousness is our original nature. To be in touch with this consciousness is the purpose of our work and life.

In the evolution of human consciousness, human intellect arrived a little later than instinct. As civilizations emerged from jungles and forests and developed into city-states, the human mind began to function more out of psychological memory than biological or natural memory. The mind of human beings was divorced from the mind of nature. The intellect, which functioned primarily from psychological memory, slowly overshadowed instinct, the origin of which was natural and biological memory. With the intellect becoming the more reliable guide for thought and action, the instinctual intelligence of our consciousness was used less and less.

CONSCIOUSNESS AS THE FIELD OF INTELLIGENCE

Consciousness connects the diversity of existence into a unified expression. Imagine the human body which is composed of several trillion cells (heart cells, brain cells, stomach cells), each of which is a separate unit of life. Yet each of these cells functions in harmony with the other cells. When the brain cells 'think' that the body is hungry, the stomach cells 'feel' the same hunger. It is as if a wave of intelligence unites the brain cells and the stomach cells into the experience of hunger. In other words, the brain cells have the consciousness of hunger just as the stomach cells do.

When we transfer this analogy to the realm of a complex and modern organization, we realize that a similar wave of intelligence connects one unit of the organization with another. Otherwise, the organization would not survive as one entity. The marketing unit must have an awareness of what the manufacturing unit is creating. The planning department must 'think' on the same wavelength with the worker on the shop floor who has a 'feel' for what the future holds for the company. The greater the flow of intelligence within the organization, the greater is the likelihood that the organization will function effectively and smoothly. The emergence

KARMA SUTRAS

of cross-functional teams in the context of industrial organizations clearly indicates that the corporations of the 21st century will try to harness the flow of intelligence within their constituent units. In short, the corporations of tomorrow will try to become more and more conscious of themselves.

We are the cosmos made conscious and life is the means by which the universe understands itself.

—Brian Cox

FOUR STATES OF SELF-CONSCIOUSNESS

The classical psychology of India describes these following four states of human consciousness:

1. The waking state or *jagrat*
2. The dream state or *swapna*
3. The dreamless-sleep state or *sushupti*
4. The state of pure consciousness or *turiya*

Jagrat is the ordinary waking and thinking state of consciousness. It is the state in which most of us spend our waking hours. In *jagrat*, we comprehend the world through the structure of conscious thoughts. Our understanding of reality in this state is primarily sensory reality processed by our five sense organs. Because our sense organs are limited in their ability to process all the reality in our environment, our waking state can give us only a fragmented view or understanding of things.

Swapna is the dream state of our consciousness. Although dreams may appear very unreal from the point of view of our waking state, they are, nevertheless, very real in the context of our dream bodies. We have to understand that dreams do not take place in an imaginary sphere outside ourselves. We experience the sensation of our dreams in our psychophy-siological structures. For instance, we have cold sweat when we have nightmares. We also experience real movement of our limbs when we encounter an accident in our dream. In the dream state, the subconscious experiences of our waking state are acted out in the language of dreams. The dream language is a metaphorical language that does not obey the logic of ordinary language. This language, however, is as real in its context as any other language; the only problem is that we seem to lack the skill to interpret it. Most tribal cultures have ways of interpreting dreams of different kinds. In modern times, many scientists have found clues to their inventions and discoveries in the dream state. In the sphere of management, too, the possibility of exploring the dream state for insights into effective decision-making was studied by Dr Francis Menezes of the House of Tatas, the largest industrial house of India.

Sushupti is the state of deep sleep. Ordinarily, we equate the state of deep sleep with a state of unconsciousness. Classical Indian psychology, however, considers *sushupti* a profound state of self-consciousness. Take the example of a person who says, 'I had such deep and blissful sleep that I was not aware of anything.' Two interpretations emerge from this statement. First, the person was not aware of anything that disturbed the sleep. Second, at the same time, the person had the awareness or experience of a blissful state in which they slept soundly. Unless there existed an experiencer of the blissful state, how can the person remember it when they are awake?

Turiya is a transcendental state of consciousness. It is not an exclusive state like the states of waking, dreaming and sleeping. It is an inclusive state, which is also present in the other three states. *Turiya* is pure consciousness, which forms the substratum of all other states of consciousness. In the words of Ramana Maharshi, '*Turiya* is another name for the Self. Aware of the waking, dream, and sleep states, we remain unaware of

KARMA SUTRAS

our own Self. Nevertheless, the Self is here and now. It is the only Reality.' *Turiya* is the ground reality of consciousness. It is the field of awareness, the ultimate quest of all our knowledge and experience. The Indian masters identified *Turiya* with higher self or, simply, the Self.

THE LEADER AS THE HERO: THE TRANSFORMATION OF CONSCIOUSNESS

Heroes transcend the limitations of the intellect to attain the power of nature from which our minds separate us. The power of heroic leadership cannot be grasped with the intellect alone; it has to be felt. One is reminded again of Gandhi's words: 'I know that ultimately one is guided not by the intellect but by the heart. The heart accepts a conclusion for which the intellect subsequently finds reasoning.' Managerial leadership that aspires to heroism must, sometimes, suspend the calculations of the intellect and go by the convictions of the heart.

Consciousness is, therefore, the edge that separates the mediocre from the heroic. This consciousness is the gateway to our own mystery and the passport to our ultimate possibility. Vedantic psychology tells us that the ultimate source of human consciousness is a centre of bliss and absolute peace. The Sanskrit word for such a state is *ananda*. It is a state beyond conscious thought, a place of absolute stillness amid the stress and turmoil of daily life. *Ananda* is not an otherworldly state. We all have experienced it at some time or another. Basketball players in championship form find the centre of quietude from which all their actions flow effortlessly and flawlessly. So do the greatest musicians and the greatest painters. A leader who has had a revelation or experience of this state of consciousness finds the secret of their peak performance.

THE MIDDLE PATH: THE WAY OF RIGHT PERCEPTION

The gospel of Buddha emphasizes right livelihood as one of the secrets of a happy life. The leadership journey is, essentially, a search for right livelihood through right perception. What, then, is the secret of right livelihood and right perception? For this, we turn to *The Dialogues of Plato*, in which the great Greek master records the following dialogue between Socrates and Adeimantus on the reason for the deterioration in the quality of life.

> Socrates: There seem to be two causes of the deterioration of the arts.
>
> Adeimantus: What are they?
>
> Socrates: Wealth, I said, and poverty.
>
> Adeimantus: How do they act?
>
> Socrates: The process is as follows: When a potter becomes rich, will he, think you, any longer take the same pains with his art?
>
> Adeimantus: Certainly not.
>
> Socrates: He will grow more and more indolent and careless?
>
> Adeimantus: Very true.
>
> Socrates: And the result will be that he becomes a worse potter?
>
> Adeimantus: Yes; he greatly deteriorates.

Socrates: But, on the other hand, if he has no money, and cannot provide himself with tools or instruments, he will not do equally well with himself, nor will he teach his sons or apprentices to work equally well.

Adeimantus: Certainly not.

Socrates: Then, under the influence, either of poverty or of wealth, workmen and their work are equally liable to degenerate?

Adeimantus: This is evident.

Socrates: Here, then, is a discovery of new evils, I said, against which the guardians will have to watch, or they will creep into the city unobserved.

Adeimantus: What evils?

Socrates: Wealth, I said, and poverty; the one is the parent of luxury and indolence and the other of meanness and viciousness, and both of discontent. (Plato, IV, 421-B)

This dialogue puts us in touch with the way a great leader arrives at the middle path of right perception. Socrates' perceptive of wisdom neither glorifies nor vilifies wealth or poverty. The Greek master takes our awareness beyond the objective world of poverty and wealth to the subjective world of wealth consciousness and poverty consciousness. He suggests that a consciousness obsessed with thoughts of either wealth or poverty is the source of discontent. The way out is to find the Golden Mean in the realm of consciousness, whereby neither wealth nor poverty can affect our quality of life.

LEADERSHIP AND COSMOCENTRIC CONSCIOUSNESS

Talking about his transformational journey towards becoming a world leader, Gandhi once said, 'There comes a time when an individual becomes irresistible and his action becomes all-pervasive in its effect. This comes when he reduces himself to zero.' Gandhi's words may appear strange or inexplicable to leaders who tend to measure power on the basis of titles, designations, qualifications, perks, pay cheques and grand self-images. Yet when we examine Gandhi's statement with the objectivity of a scientist, we realize its validity.

First, let us understand what Gandhi means by the expression 'reduces himself to zero'. Ordinarily, the symbol '0' gives us an impression of nothingness. Yet we know that zero is a powerful entity in the world of mathematics.

A zero can fundamentally alter the quantitative and qualitative value of any given number. Zero is, indeed, the domain of infinite potentiality.

In India, where this symbol is supposed to have originated, the zero is known as *shunnyo* or the 'void'. The great Indian minds were not content with using zero as a symbol or a concept. They wanted to understand '0' as a real experience. Buddha's experience of nirvana was nothing but the qualitative experience of zero. The Buddhists call it *shunnyata*. This was Buddha's experience of the field of consciousness free of objects. Therefore, '0' is a powerful metaphor for the reality of our existence.

As we move from the philosophical to the experiential understanding of '0', we realize why Gandhi urged us to reduce ourselves to zero. When we closely examine our self-concepts, we realize that all that we imagine we are revolves around the centre of our ego. A state of zero is simply the absence of our divisive ego. This ego separates us from the greater amplitude of our consciousness.

Reducing the ego to zero helps us to progress from egocentric personality to what we may call 'cosmocentric individuality'. Cosmocentricity places individuals in harmonious relation with the laws of nature. If we look deeply into all the phenomena of nature, we can see cosmocentric consciousness at work.

Leaders are in touch with the creative rhythm of cosmic consciousness. The leader-follower relationship is one of the unity of consciousness. The Sanskrit word for this is *ekatmanubhuti* or the feeling of unity. Leadership and followership cannot be differentiated in a state of *ekatmanubhuti*. They merge in the common ground of unity of consciousness.

LEADERSHIP AS A STATE OF CONSCIOUSNESS

Lao tzu, China's most influential sage and political ruler in the 5th century BC, had astute insights into the process of effective leadership.

In Lao Tzu's hierarchy of leadership, the foremost quality of a leader is to be conscious of the leadership potential of the followers and to let them use this potential in a spontaneous way. According to him, when a great leader accomplishes this task with effortless ease, the followers say, 'We did it ourselves.' Lao Tzu was talking about the process of empowerment, which is often misunderstood in the context of corporate leadership.

Empowerment is not about giving power to the other in the physical sense of the term. It is about energizing and developing the source of power that the other already possesses. A staff member in research and development may not necessarily be empowered if given higher managerial responsibility in the organization. On the other hand, they may feel truly empowered if one of the products that they designed is given recognition by the organization. Max De Pree of the furniture company Herman Miller in a *Fortune*-magazine interview said:

> Take a 33-year-old man who assembles chairs. He's been doing it several years. He has a wife and two children. He knows what to do when the children have earaches, and how to get them through school. He probably serves on a volunteer board. And when he comes to work we give him a supervisor. He doesn't need one. His problem isn't to be supervised; it's to continue toward reaching his potential. (Chatterjee 1998, 55)

Empowering leadership is a conscious process of capacity building, that is, recognizing capacity and developing it. Goethe described this process beautifully: 'If you treat an individual as he is, he will remain as he is. But if you treat him as if he were what he ought to be and could be, he will become what he ought to be and could be.'

✳ **8** ✳

WORKSHIP

Believe you can and you're halfway there.

—Theodore Roosevelt

THE MISSING LINK: SPIRIT IN ACTION

Our industrial civilization has superimposed its own limitations on the cosmic field of action. It has narrowed our view of work to an economically driven, production-focused activity that, apparently, has no link with the nature and spirit of our being.

Most of our dialogues and discussions concerning our work, surprisingly, bypass or overlook this spiritual dimension of work and its role in setting right the existential vacuum that afflicts most workers in the modern age.

Let us examine the etymological roots of the following expressions found in the vocabulary of industrial organizations as evidence of what I am trying to convey.

- Professional management
- Charismatic leadership
- *Esprit de corps*
- Team spirit
- Organizational mission

All great leaders nurture their inner spirits in silence and solitude. They are unwavering in their commitment to their chosen ideals. Like Martin Luther King Jr, they all nourish their dreams. After years of inner preparation, when they emerge on to the public arena of life, their indomitable spirit carries them forward.

WORKSHIP: WORK AS WORSHIP

To convey the spiritual essence of an action, the ancient psychologists of India often used a word that does not have a literal translation in English. The word they used was *karmayoga*. This compound word loosely means 'work that is linked with the transcendental spirit.' My futile search for an equivalent expression in English has prompted me to use the word 'workship'.

Three teachers, who teach history in different schools are asked the same question: What is your present job? The first one replies, 'I don't do very much. I just teach history to schoolchildren.' The second teacher thinks a little more deeply and says, 'I am in the business of education.' The third teacher, in response to the same question, looks straight into the eyes of the questioner and, in an inspired voice, says, 'I am shaping the destiny of the nation. I teach young minds how they can make history.

All three teachers are dealing with the same reality—teaching history to schoolchildren. Yet the spirit in which they approach their work transforms the mundane reality of their job. It is this transformational power of the spirit of our work that leads us to the expression 'workship'.

LEADERSHIP WORK: AN ADVENTURE OF CONSCIOUSNESS

The essence of leadership work is to bring about a transformation in the consciousness of the leader that gives them a new standpoint for undertaking and directing action. As described by Patanjali, an ancient sage, this is a liberating process that gives the leader a taste of *mukti* (freedom) and *ananda* (joy), which, as the Upanishads tell us, are the highest goals of all work. Mundane work becomes workship when action is linked to transcendental consciousness.

When we stop thinking primarily about our limited selves and our own conveniences, we undergo a truly heroic transformation of consciousness. The Upanishads explore this transformational journey in terms of four stages of development of self to the Self. These four stages of self-development do not take place in mutually exclusive compartments but overlap in a continuum that forms the mosaic of human consciousness.

The first stage of the self, according to the Upanishads, is *annamaya kosha* or the physical self made of food. From the standpoint of work, the physical self concerns itself with basic physical needs, such as food and shelter. This provides an obvious rationale for work for most human beings.

The second stage is that of the vital self. The Upanishads call this *pranamaya kosha*. A worker at this level of consciousness desires to bring about an extension of the field of physical activity by means of group affiliation and a sense of belongingness to a larger identity, such as a family or an organization.

The third stage of human consciousness is *manamaya kosha*, or the mental self. This self concerns itself with intellectual and aesthetically satisfying activity, such as highly skilled work or artistic pursuits.

The last stage of the self, as described by the Upanishads, is the *vigyanamaya kosha*, which is the sheath of intelligence. This self encompasses the psychic and spiritual domains of human consciousness.

In the last stage of its journey towards higher consciousness, the self of the leader begins to glimpse the Self. The newly awakened consciousness liberates the leader from their limited notion of themselves as a physical, vital, mental frame and transports them to the realm of freedom and joy.

THE FOURFOLD PATHS OF WORKSHIP

There are fourfold paths to leadership work, four roadmaps as it were, all of which take the leader towards 'workship'. All these are inner paths leading to the same destination, which is the Self.

DISCIPLINE

Discipline is the first path towards workship. In the context of modern organizations, discipline has become synonymous with rules and regulations, legalities and procedures.

RIGHTEOUSNESS

Righteousness is the next path towards effective action. Ordinarily, righteousness means ethically right action. Righteous action, however, is not merely superficial morality. In its true sense, righteous action means acting according to the law of one's being, which the Bhagavad Gita describes as *swadharma*.

SACRIFICE

Sacrifice is the third dimension of leadership work. This word has acquired a negative connotation in everyday usage.

However, the sacrifice that we are talking about in the context of leadership work does not diminish the self but extends the boundary of the self by giving up the lower for the cause of the higher.

TRANSCENDENCE

Transcendence is the final step in workship. This is a state of realization in action. What do leaders realize in the middle of action? They cannot realize that which does not exist in reality. What leaders can and do realize is a higher order of reality of their own Selves.

Leaders can comprehend the emergence of great principles in, apparently, small things. They see larger processes behind small events. This happens because they have experienced transcendence in their own lives. They have seen life as a uniting principle beyond the dualities of pleasure and pain, success and failure, worker and work. A quiet, still wisdom dawns on these leaders as they realize that they are instruments of a larger purpose of life. The Bhagavad Gita describes this state of transcendence as *nirdwanda stithaprajna*, a state of equilibrium of consciousness beyond the stress and dualities of work life. In Shintoism, the Oracle of Sumiyoshi describes the transcendental state of a leader in these beautiful lines:

> *I have no corporeal existence*
> *But universal benevolence is my divine body.*
> *I have no physical power*
> *But uprightness is my strength.*
> *I have no religious clairvoyance beyond*
> *What is bestowed by wisdom.*
> *I have no power of miracle other than*
> *The attainment of quiet happiness.*
> *I have no tact except*
> *The exercise of gentleness.* (Chatterjee 2008, 55)

IS WORKSHIP WORKABLE?

Workship not only is a philosophical construct but also is based on experiential learning and collective wisdom of many men and women of the world. Gandhi and Mother Teresa are not quirks of history. They are part of a glorious continuum of people throughout history who have, time and again, shown us the efficacy of workship as an alternative to the need- and greed-based contemporary models of work.

Japan has demonstrated a national model of workship. Much of modern scholarship tends to explain the Japanese economic miracle in terms of stereotypes such as pan-nationalism, work culture, kaizen and total quality management.

In the global context, we find that a consumption-based model of work poses a serious threat to the viability of our ecological and environmental system. Workship is a leader's adventure of consciousness. Like all adventures, the path leading to the final destination offers surprises at every turn—pleasures and pitfalls, failures and successes—which make all journeys memorable. All adventures are unique, just as all human beings are unique, although they have a common ancestry and a common destiny in birth and death. Yet, imagine a leader's surprise when they discover, after years of travelling, that their destination was never apart from them but always was a part of their very being, resting deep within themselves, only waiting to be arrived at by means of the magic wings of awareness.

Effortless effort is a function of an integral being. Gandhi was known to be able to sustain a high level of energy for long periods of time. Most leaders seem to possess an inexhaustible storehouse of energy and a great capacity for action. This is possible because a great leader is able to focus their entire energy on the process of action without losing sight of the larger goal at the same time. Swami Vivekananda once said, 'Pay attention to the means of work. The end will take care of itself.'

Effortless effort is nothing but the science and art of energy conservation. Take this example from the corporate world. Two managers, X and Y, are competing for a particular leadership position in a corporation. X is very goal-oriented. He is highly imaginative and dreams of his impending success. He is obsessed with the prospect of his promotion and is very anxious to know whether he would be promoted at the end of the year. In contrast, Y is introspective. She concentrates more on her work rather than on its possible outcome. She is not as power-driven as X but is intensely focused on her work. She would also like to assume the position that X is aspiring for, but she does not obsess about it. Now, let us explore the possible psychological states of X and Y under the following circumstances.

Circumstance No. 1—X is promoted instead of Y: In this circumstance, X will be thrilled as his dream has come true. He is likely to thump his chest proudly and raise his arms like a football star and exult, 'I did it!' Y will be disappointed, of course. But since she did not invest too much psychological energy in achieving the goal, she will be sad for a while and then resume her work, saying, 'I must work harder and find out where my deficiencies are.'

Circumstance No. 2—Y is promoted instead of X: In this case, X's world is likely to come crashing down. He had pinned a great deal of hope on this promotion, had invested considerable psychological energy in it (fantasizing how happy his wife would be, how he would spend the extra money on a new car, and so on). He is furious with his boss for not promoting him and remains sullen and angry with his colleagues for many days. On the other hand, Y is happy with her promotion. But since her focus had been more on her work, she tells herself, 'I must have done my job well. However, I must do even better in the future.'

Circumstance No. 3—Neither X nor Y is promoted: We have already discussed the impact of failure on X and Y. It is clear that since Y is more focused on the process rather than on the outcome, she is more likely to handle failure better and is also better equipped to face further challenges than X.

Leaders are the ones who bring a surge of energy and a sense of rhythm into the arena of action. The execution of their work has the flawlessness of one of nature's masterpieces. Leaders excel because of the quality of their service. The only ones among us who will be truly fulfilled in our work are those who have sought the way to serve others and found it. The search for a true vocation is to learn how we can best serve the world. Leadership is a natural outcome of this search.

✳ 9 ✳

ORGANIZATION

Nature uses only the longest threads to weave her patterns, so that each small piece of her fabric reveals the organization of the entire tapestry.

—Richard P. Feynman

THE ALCHEMY OF COLLABORATION

The story of organizations is to be found in nature's manuscript, the unwritten book of nature that scripts, in vivid detail, the fundamental quest of all life forms to manifest their fullest potential for collective action.

A honeycomb is a realization of the organizational instinct inherent in bees. The basic design of the honeycomb is an intricate hexagonal structure that slopes at a precise angle of 13 degrees to the horizontal. It is an act of sophisticated civil engineering that prevents honey from running out of the hive. Bees also demonstrate the air-conditioning mechanism implicit in natural intelligence by crowding themselves into a dense mass when the honeycomb is made. The temperature of this mass is held constant between 34° C and 35° C, which is necessary for the secretion of wax. All these things happen as the unerring instinct of the bee begins to orchestrate itself with the laws of nature. The honeycomb is not a building that has been laboriously constructed brick by brick. It is an outcome of spontaneous creation, a piece of brilliant architecture that emerges from the blueprint of conscious nature.

The functioning of the human body is another example of this kind of alchemy at work. The various organs of the body, such as the heart, the liver, and the kidneys, serve as the hubs of activity within a particular system. In short, everything that constitutes the organization of the body is geared towards one organizational goal—to maintain the body in a state of health. The body achieves this goal through a unique process known as homeostasis.

Even a minuscule increase in the sugar or salt level or the temperature of the body is capable of upsetting the person's health. Yet the human organism maintains its resilience against all odds through the principle of homeostasis.

In many ways, organizations resemble the working of the human body. The theory of organization as an organism is not a new one. But most sociological studies in this respect have ignored the invisible element of conscious intelligence that pervades any organization or organism. Synergy in human organizations is an outcome of group dynamics in much the same way as the dynamic interaction of a group of bees brings about the energy and intelligence required to create a beehive.

ORGANIZATION AS A COMMUNITY

Corporations and communities may exist for different purposes, but the common ground between them is that they are made up of human beings; they are run by human beings; and they are meant to serve human needs and aspirations. Human beings do not live only on the basis of lateral relationships with their peers and superiors at work. They search for the vertical purpose of their existence in this grand cosmic scheme of things of which they form an integral part.

KARMA SUTRAS

In modern corporations, leaders are seen primarily as strategists whose sole aim seems to be to outwit rival companies to stay in business. Policies and not principles seem to be the guiding light for this kind of leadership. CEOs continue to earn astronomical salaries even when they downsize employees in the name of austerity measures. Gandhi, who himself led with principles, once said that leading with policies is not an authentic test of leadership because if a leader says that 'honesty is the best policy', he implies that if it were not the best policy, under certain circumstances, he would abandon honesty. If modern corporations acknowledge the fact that they are like traditional communities in more ways than one, then we will begin to see a new tradition emerging in business.

ORGANIZATIONS: FROM CONSTRUCTION TO CREATION

In trying to understand the nature of human organizations, one ought to make a distinction between creation and construction. Where creation is a living process, construction is a finished or unfinished structure of frozen life. Creation is multidimensional and dynamic; construction is sequential, progressing step by step. A tree growing from a seed is creation; a building rising from its foundation is construction.

Any human organization has both a creative aspect and a constructive aspect. Whereas the energy and vision of its members constitute the creative element of an organization, the functional division of the organization into design, manufacturing and marketing constitutes the constructive element.

Managers are often tempted to tamper with the constructive elements of the organization, but they do so to an excessive degree. The reason is obvious; it gives greater visibility to their management functions and brings greater rewards.

A designer is obsessed with an exotic design that will show him as a performer irrespective of the value of the design to the organization. Similarly, a production manager is fixated on achieving certain production figures, but without bothering to find out whether it is possible to make better-quality products within the given parameters.

LEADERSHIP IN A LEARNING ORGANIZATION

Learning is as old as civilization itself. When human beings first learned to use fire, an entirely new vista of possibilities for action opened up to civilization. In the context of leadership, learning may be described as building capacity for action. This capacity for action does not come merely from knowledge; it comes from learning. We must differentiate between knowledge and learning. Knowledge is the process of accumulating information or experience in a given context. Thus, knowledge is an event. Learning, on the other hand, is the movement of knowledge beyond an event. Learning is a continuous process. Take the discovery of fire by a certain member of the human species on a particular day. This discovery did not end in an event in which one person acquired the knowledge of how to start a fire. Rather, this event triggered in the consciousness of this one person's knowledge about a process of making further discoveries. Knowledge about the event of starting a fire gives rise to new learnings about the multiple capacities of fire to ignite, illuminate, generate power and destroy.

Learning is not merely capacity building; it is capacity building in one's self. Learning is the process of self-knowing. Knowledge of external reality is merely a stimulus.

To draw on the example of learning to ride a bicycle, we can see that this learning is a self-generating process. As we learn the generic skill of balancing ourselves on two wheels and propelling ourselves forward, we acquire the capacity of riding not only a bicycle but also a motorcycle or, for that matter, anything that requires this ability to hold the body in a dynamic balance.

Leaders acquire the discipline to operationalize knowledge into learning. Their learning is synonymous with action. When Gandhi was 35 years of age and living in South Africa, he came across a book called *Unto This Last* by John Ruskin. Ruskin wrote that the liberation of the individual lay in the liberation of the community. This single book transformed Gandhi's life and he resolved to convert this knowledge into action.

The sages of India understood that the ultimate quest of all learning is self-learning. They called this process *swadhyay*. Self-learning is a never-ending process of discovering the foundation of all knowledge.

ORGANIZATIONAL VALUES AND SELF-LEARNING

In the fast-changing knowledge economies of the 21st century, self-learning will be a core competency and continuous learning the only way to survive global competitiveness.

In the next few pages, I discuss humility, faith and total quality consciousness as the three foundational values of learning.

HUMILITY

The first step in learning is humility. It is the ground on which knowledge grows into learning. The word humility comes from humus or soil. The ground reality or the soil is a state of pure potentiality.

There is a radical difference between the two ways of looking at humility. In the first instance, when we underplay our own importance because that is the expected social norm, we are being humble in the conventional and more-acceptable sense of the word. In this case, we may assume an appearance of humility before others, but we can still be full of thoughts about ourselves and our own importance. On the other hand, if we are truly humble, we learn to reduce the energy and time that we invest in thinking about our own accomplishments and in bolstering our own egos. When we take stock of how much organizational time and energy goes to waste in holding on to our positions and points of view, we realize that we hardly have any energy or time left to learn anything new.

FAITH

The second important value on which a learning organization is built is faith or trust. Trust is only a consequence of faith. Organizations such as the Missionaries of Charity, The Salvation Army, and the Ramakrishna Mission are built purely on faith. Truly speaking, no organization can survive, let alone learn, without faith. I have often asked these questions of myself: Is there any one thing I have learned in my life that did not begin with faith? How did I learn the alphabet? Because I had faith in my parents, whom I trusted. How did I learn mathematics and geography? I had faith in my teachers. I still learn new things simply because I have faith in my ability to learn.

TOTAL QUALITY CONSCIOUSNESS

The third organizational value that facilitates self-learning is total quality consciousness. Total quality management has so far looked into the issue of job enrichment by bringing greater refinement to products, systems and processes on the job. However, it has, often, neglected the issue of self-learning through quality consciousness.

Quality consciousness comes from the quality of attention that we bring to any job in which we are engaged. When our attention to any task is total, we discover a certain magical quality about our work.

Leaders learn from moment-to-moment in a process of self-referral. Their learning today is not conditioned by the knowledge of yesterday. They have a freshness, receptivity and agility of mind to absorb new learning. While most of us become the prisoners of our experience, leaders stay in touch with the active present. They learn not from memory but from the present moment. Their selves expand in the sheer joy of learning. Their delight in learning bubbles over the confines of their own selves and lights up the minds of their co-workers.

True learning is like lighting a lamp. You can light a thousand fires from the same lamp without diminishing the flame of the original. Enlightened leaders are like the first lamp. They generate an inexhaustible source of learning in the organization without, in any way, diminishing the light that shines through them.

10

COMMUNICATION

In the attitude of silence the soul finds the path in a clearer light, and what is elusive and deceptive resolves itself into crystal clearness. Our life is a long and arduous quest after Truth.

—**Mahatma Gandhi**

SILENCE AS A LANGUAGE

Silence is the womb of language. Silence conceives, prepares and gives birth to language. Just as the noisy surface of the sea is held together by the vast, unruffled depths of water, silence integrates language into meaning and understanding.

Communication through language happens as a result of an exchange or transaction of meaning. The law of exchange is based on a common value assigned to the objects being exchanged. If we were to exchange dollars for yen, the common value would be the purchasing power of the currency. Similarly, in an exchange of words, the common value is silence. All words can be reconverted into silence; they emerge from silence and merge into silence.

To understand how words are created from silence, try this experiment in the following sequence:

1. Take any word that you can pronounce comfortably, for example, leader, and utter it aloud 10 times.

2. Close your lips and utter the same word in your mind for a minute. You will experience a distinct vibration of the word leader in your mind.
3. Keep your lips closed and your eyes shut for a couple of minutes immediately after the second step. Do not think of anything, in particular, but pay attention to whatever comes to your mind. A very faint vibration of the word leader will persist somewhere deep in the cellular structure of your mind. If you are alert enough, you will experience how the vibration merges into silence.

One of the important issues in leadership development is the ability to make the right choices. A leader has to make many significant choices in the course of their life and work. A wise leader knows that choices are made in the space and time that exist between a certain stimulus and an appropriate response. For example, a business leader working for an insurance company is faced with a dilemma; she has to decide within five minutes whether she should insure a particular business. She has collected all the relevant data relating to this particular business and studied it carefully. Yet she is indecisive; she is unable to figure out whether it will be good business or bad business for her company. As she debates over the pros and cons of the two possible choices before her, time is running out. At this point, she sits in silence with her eyes closed and ponders deeply. Then she makes the decision.

LEADERSHIP AND THE ART OF LISTENING

Mahavira, a contemporary of Buddha, was an enlightened master who founded the religion known as Jainism. Mahavira talked about the way of the *shravaka*, or the listener, as a path towards enlightenment. Listening was valued in the sacred traditions because it was synonymous with learning.

We learn more deeply through our ears than through our eyes. Our eyes only skim the surface of reality as a succession of forms. The eyes are very linear in their reception of images. While listening, we absorb information from multiple directions. That is why when we think deeply about something, we tend to close our eyes and listen more through our ears.

When leaders listen, they first pay attention to their inner impulses. By doing so, they establish communication with their own selves. They bring to the light of consciousness the background noise created by their own voices. Once this noise has settled down, true listening begins. Otherwise, the leader imposes their own voice on the voice of the person to whom they are listening.

Listening, like language, has more than one dimension. First, there is the 'dimension of the factual'. At this level, language is merely a statement of fact. For example, when someone informs us that it rained last weekend or that a company has increased its profits by 10 per cent, we listen to statements of fact.

The second dimension of language is the 'dimension of the intentional'. At this level, one has to listen to the more subtle intent behind what a speaker says. When a boss tells a subordinate, 'I appreciate your coming to the office on time today', she is conveying a different message from what the mere words would seem to communicate.

The third and the most subtle dimension of language is the 'transformational dimension'. Language has a certain alchemy that can transform the heart and mind of the listener. This transformation comes about in the listener through a process known as 'empathy'.

Deep listening facilitates the flow of intelligence in communication by removing the physical, physiological and mental barriers that separate the speaker from the listener.

Rumi (1995) said:

> A tongue has one customer, the ear.

The relation between the tongue and the ear is not like a mechanical relation between one organ of the body and another. It is not as though the tongue pours out information and the ear receives it. Leaders know that the purpose of listening is to create not eloquence but understanding. They follow Shakespeare's dictum: 'Give every man thy ear, but few thy voice' (*Hamlet*, Act I, Scene 3; William 2008).

WORDS: HOW THEY SHAPE OUR WORLD

The word is not a human invention. Nor is it a mere tool of communication; it is infinitely more. It does not, merely, convey an empty sound or a rational idea devoid of power.

All words exist in seed form as sound. In this form, the word is a conscious but undifferentiated principle. Then the sound becomes differentiated in the mind and takes the form of a thought. Finally, it becomes articulate speech as it passes through different organs of articulation such as the larynx, tongue, palate, teeth and lips.

In the seed form, the word, as a sound, is nothing but conscious energy. At this stage, the word does not acquire audibility or amplitude and is, merely, an intention. Under the impulse of perception, this conscious energy of intention creates a nervous tension in the mind that seeks release through speech.

Natural forms and phenomena create the deep structure of words. In the course of history, words derived from nature came to acquire material forms that are almost divorced from their source of origin. The word trade now means to do business. Originally, this word meant a recurring habit or manner in life or a path traversed, as in 'treading a path'. From this, it acquired the restricted meaning of work or a profession.

The difference between a tree and a stone is merely a qualitative difference in the vibration of the same atoms. The word stands as a bridge between the vibration of the natural world, which is things, and the vibration of the mental world, which is thoughts. The process of the conversion of thoughts into things, and vice versa, happens through the word. The Gospel of St John says about this process: 'In the beginning was the Word.... The Word was made flesh' (1:1, 14).

Leaders bring to their words a certain consciousness of the spirit behind the utterances. Before leaders greet you 'good morning', they experience the goodness of the morning in themselves. They shake your hand, look straight into your eyes, take a deep breath, bring their attention to the words that come from the depths of their heart, and say, 'Good morning.' You do not so much hear the words as you hear the conviction in the leader's voice and feel the energy of their words. This is the secret of high-touch leadership.

PROBLEM SOLVING: LIVING IN QUESTIONS

To integrate the many ways of looking at a problem, the leader has to live in questions. A leader who believes in giving quick fix answers is, more often than not, compounding the problem. The quick fix solution itself multiplies the problem into two parts. One part can be remedied with a clean-up operation, and the other part can be pushed under the carpet temporarily. That which is pushed under the carpet, however, triggers a new set of problems, the magnitude of which may be incalculable. To solve the 'problem' of a crying child, a mother provides a quick fix solution: Give the child whatever they want. This pacifies the child momentarily and the crying stops. A new problem arises with this kind of an expedient solution, because the child does not learn the discipline of patience. This new problem is compounded as the child grows in years and is likely to develop an abusive and intemperate personality.

If a question is held long enough in the consciousness of the questioner, this very act brings the questioner to a heightened state of awareness. A question is nothing but the concentration of energy on an aspect of our reality that appears foggy to us. The more intense the questioning, the greater is the concentration of energy on the fogginess of the reality.

Leadership is a quest and not a fixed target. A leader lives in questions and not in answers. The *Brihadaranyaka Upanishad* describes the quest of a leader in an elegant phrase: *neti neti charaibeti*, not here, not here, move on. This relentless movement of the leader is a movement in the realm of consciousness. While making the journey, leaders discover that today's problem is a result of yesterday's solution. The response to this discovery is greater receptivity and the beginning of a dialogue with themselves. In a dialogue, there is no final solution; there is only the flow of intelligence through the recesses of the mind. When intelligence flows, a problem need not be solved; it simply dissolves by itself.

COMMUNICATION: A TRYST WITH TRUTH

Reuben Mark, a successful CEO of Colgate Palmolive told *Fortune* magazine, 'You've got to be honest and straightforward: What you tell the outside world has to be the same thing you tell your senior people, and the same thing you tell your factory workers.' While this may sound like a cliché, all leaders realize, in the short or the long run, that the foundation of effective communication is authentic communication.

Leadership communication is a tryst with the truth. By truth, I mean not merely an absence of lies but an active pursuit of what is real in the ultimate sense. Gandhi said, 'Truth is my god.' His experiment with the truth was nothing but the pursuit, with uncompromising zeal, of the ultimate natural law that animates all forms and phenomena of nature. At the end of his journey, Gandhi discovered that there is no way to find the truth except through the way of non-violence. Every leader discovers his or her way of seeking out truth. But the ultimate result is the same: A life that communicates the power and passion of authentic living. It is only then that the leader can say, 'My life is my message.'

In the final analysis, character in communication comes when we say only what we believe can be realized. This means that we need to learn the discipline of not speaking thoughtlessly. This also means that we should neither praise too highly nor blame too excessively. Leaders learn to communicate with a consciousness that their words are capable of changing the destinies of the people with whom they are communicating.

* 11 *

HUMAN VALUES

The greatest danger in times of turbulence is not the turbulence—it is to act with yesterday's logic.

—Peter Drucker

TRADITION AND TRANSFORMATION: FROM METAPHOR TO METAMORPHOSIS

Tradition, like statistics, has a way of discovering reality. In statistics, we all know that the larger the sample size—that is, the greater the spread of data collected—the closer is the sample to reality. In the context of various traditions, the farther a tradition goes back in time, the greater is the chance that it is telling you deeper truths about the realities of human existence.

Traditions are built on the basis of and held together by some values that are like social contracts. These values are not as tangible as the constitution of a country; they are codified in human behaviour and rituals and are passed down from generation to generation.

The process of modernization, sometimes, brings about modification in culture-specific values. For example, in traditional Indian culture, the son was identified with the father's profession. In contemporary India, however, this value has weakened considerably. In Asian societies that frowned upon women working outside the home and where women's traditional role was confined to the household, we are witnessing the increasing feminization of the workforce. But traditions go much deeper than societal values. Traditions evolve from the lived experiences of individuals about certain truths of life, that is, how to conduct oneself in one's own life in order to function effectively and harmoniously with others. These truths are then accepted and codified as values, norms and rituals by members of society.

Traditions undergo change not because the truths they uphold are no longer valid. Human beings, by their very nature, are creative beings. They are always looking for new ways of arriving at the same goal. To bring about human transformation, all traditions have to be made contemporary. They have to be lived over and over again before their value begins to unfold. In the absence of lived experience, traditions are reduced to the empty shells of mindless rules.

When organizations become rigid, they merely ritualize tradition. When they are dynamic, they enliven tradition into evolving into newer forms and capacities.

Leaders transform organizations not by imitating other successful organizations but by looking deeply within the traditions of their own organizations. They listen to the voices of the people who have been there for some time, pay attention to the success stories these long-time employees tell, the reasons they ascribe to failures, the aspirations they articulate and the values they cherish. Leaders simply energize and facilitate the spontaneous flowering of indigenous ideas within the organization. They constitute the invisible tradition of the organization. They are, indeed, the instruments for the inside-out transformation of the organization, the agents who bring about a metamorphosis.

HUMAN VALUES: THE DEEP STRUCTURE OF LEADERSHIP

In organizations, there are two types of leaders: The first follow the path of desire, and the second follow the path of the desirable. As a wit once remarked, the second type of leaders serve as the pillars of an organization, while the first type serve as caterpillars. Human values pave the path of the desirable. What, then, are human values? How are they different from any other kind of value, such as commercial value, scientific value or aesthetic value? First of all, human values constitute the deep-rooted structure of human consciousness that determine all other kinds of values—scientific, commercial and artistic.

Human values are the invisible roots of organizational values. They determine the rationale for which an organization exists. Human values are distinct from commercial values in that they are not so much guided by the will to get as they are by the will to give. Sony wants its employees 'to experience the sheer joy that comes from the advancement, application and innovation of technology that benefits the general public.' Sony thrives on the will to give its customers joy and happiness. Its will to gain a larger market share for itself is subordinated to the pursuit of larger and higher human values. In an IIM survey, conducted in 2001 among 1,000 managers in twelve Indian organizations spread throughout the country, researchers asked, 'What are some of the qualities that you look for in a leader?' The respondents gave the following as the top five attributes of a good leader:

1. Dynamism
2. Inspiring character
3. Vision
4. Ethical values
5. Spiritual strength

It was evident from the responses that Indian managers were defining leadership from the deeper perspective of core human values and not, merely, as a function of superficial skills. The core leadership values of character, spiritual strength and vision remain the cornerstone of the highest aspirations of managers. The study further revealed a cultural congruence within the Indian tradition that prompted managers from different parts of the country to subscribe to the same set of values despite differences in age, sex, language and qualification.

HIERARCHY AND THE NEW ORDER IN ORGANIZATIONS

Hierarchy is a dirty word in contemporary business. Hierarchical organizations, which still persist in many parts of the world, are looked down upon as high-fat, low-calorie and low-energy companies.

One of the most misunderstood notions about hierarchy is that it exists only in the physical structuring of an organization. In the process, we ignore the evidence of hierarchy in the psychological organization of human beings. In contemporary organizations, one hears about fast-track employees, implying that there is also a hierarchical presence of slow-track workers. There are key performance areas, which means that there are also areas in which performance may be kept at a relatively low key. In modern parlance, there may be diminishing evidence of vertical, pyramid-like organizations, but there is certainly more and more downsizing, whereby there exists an invisible hierarchy of those who can survive and those who cannot.

The evolution of human beings represents the progress of human potential. The species we know as Homo sapiens is not the final outcome of nature's evolutionary urge. The human being as we know today is only a transitional state and not a final destination.

No relationship can exist without a difference in potential. Whether it is a relationship between two metals, or between the members of a family, or between the different parts of an organization, the preconditions for any relationship include not only diversity but also a difference in potential. In Japanese organizations, senpai-kōhai is a relationship of the elder brother with the younger brother. This relationship is marked by a difference of perspective. The elder brother is not necessarily better or more able than the younger brother, but he is more responsible because he is older. The privilege of being the older brother entails greater authority but also more responsibility. He may demand obedience, but he also has to be illustrious. The younger brother treats the older brother with respect. This respect is nothing but the emotional acknowledgement of the fact that the younger brother must rise to the higher potential of the older brother.

A leader understands the organization of all forms and phenomena in nature as an interdependent play of position and perspective. Hierarchies in human organizations are just that—an amalgam of position and perspective. This is what constitutes the ground of relationships within the organization. The superior positions of leaders only give them greater perspective. Truly conscious leaders use their positions not to demand greater perquisites for themselves but to gain a better perspective of organizational reality.

SHARED VALUES: LEADERSHIP AS RELATIONSHIP

The essence of human relationships is that one does not view the other person as an object from the outside. Rather, one experiences within one's self what the other person is experiencing. This is true empathy. The Sanskrit expression for this is *Tat twam asi*, which literally means, 'I am you.' When one is in a deep relationship, the barrier between 'I' and 'you' is bridged by an inexplicable communion of the spirit. The mother feels this communion with her child, the lover feels it with his beloved, the devotee feels it with the divine, and the leader feels it with the led. In this communion, there is total abandonment of the self. In this communion alone, true communication takes place.

In building relationships within an organization, leaders do not necessarily have to bring everyone around to their point of view. This is not possible in large organizations, in which there are bound to be disagreements and dissenting voices. If leaders try to crush any opposition to their views or actions, they will only end up creating walls of resistance. By being defenceless and transparent, they disarm their opponents and adversaries, who have nothing left to attack. Gandhi overcame his opponents by appealing to and arousing what he called the 'soul-force' in them. When leaders operate from a higher reference point of conduct and action, they can relate even to those who stand against them.

Max De Pree, the retired CEO of Herman Miller, rightly said, 'You have to look at leadership through the eyes of the follower.' Leaders have the unenviable task of having to motivate and inspire a thousand minds in the pursuit of an organizational goal. How do they do that? Swami Vivekananda, a great institution builder himself, said that to do this, a leader has to be 'a servant of servants'. Conscious leaders lead from behind. By choosing to serve, they eliminate partiality, prejudice and power motives from the repertoire of their actions. Thus, they gain the moral mandate to lead, though they have come only to serve.

 KARMA SUTRAS

LEADERSHIP MOTIVATION: THE LAW OF GIVING

> Many times a day, I realize how much my own inner and outer life is built on the labors of other men, both living and dead, and how earnestly I must exert myself in order to give in return as much as I have received.

These are not the words of a saint but a scientist, Albert Einstein, whose life was a search for the eternal truths of life.

A conscious leader understands the paradox of nature, in which the law of giving functions in the reverse direction to the law of grabbing. As one grabs more money, power and status, one accumulates. As one hoards what one has accumulated, one grows poorer and poorer. This poverty is the outcome of the limiting law of material wealth. All material wealth diminishes in time and in unfavourable circumstances. The grabbing mind is forever insecure that its wealth will be taken away by someone else.

When the flower blooms, bees come to it without invitation. Leaders learn through experience that the law of giving results in the flowering of a new state of consciousness. This state of consciousness activates the affluence or the 'flowing in' of the bounty of material nature. Consciousness, which is spiritual affluence, is the primal cause, and material affluence is the consequence. Between the cause and the consequence, what operates is the mechanics of the law of giving.

Self-managed teams in contemporary organizations energize themselves by means of the principle of self-giving. For that matter, no teamwork can happen without unconditional giving by team members. Team spirit is developed when giving happens spontaneously. Mother Teresa told her sisters in the

Missionaries of Charity, 'Give till it hurts.' In organizational teamwork, members give their labour, their knowledge and their attention. They also lend their ears and voices. Finally, they give their heart and their spirit. Leadership is the task of orchestrating of the unique gifts that each team member brings to the organization. A leader's role is to turn the conditioned efforts of team members towards unconditional giving.

TAKERS, GIVERS, MATCHERS: SCIENCE OF HAPPINESS!

If you want a minute of happiness, let a spoonful of ice cream melt on your tongue. The ice cream may stay a short while on your lips but remain for a lifetime on your hips! If you truly wish for a lifetime of happiness, dissolve your ego in the service of another.

The business of happiness is not just a private affair. Happiness has become a state subject governmental concern. I was invited to visit Bhutan and Dubai once and had the privilege of meeting some of the stalwarts involved with the business of happiness. Bhutan was creating a measure of growth by substituting GDP with GNH, or gross national happiness. The United Arab Emirates appointed a new Minister of Happiness, Ms Ohood Al Roumi, whose job description was, simply, to put the happiness of citizens at the forefront of the government's priorities. Thailand is working on its own national happiness index.

Happiness has become a sizzling subject of academic as well as corporate interest all over the world. Jeffrey Sachs, a very eminent academic and director of the Earth Institute at Columbia University, says, 'Measuring self-reported happiness and achieving well-being should be on every nation's agenda as they begin to pursue the Sustainable Development Goals ....'

Adam Grant, a Wharton Business School professor, classified a large sample of people he researched in three categories: takers, givers and matchers. Here is how I would classify takers, givers and matchers. Think of a whole class of college guys going to celebrate graduation in a restaurant. The takers will expect someone else to pay for their food, the givers will be the first ones to offer to pay for everyone. The matchers will want to go Dutch so that everyone shares equally. Grant's startling research finding demonstrates this: Givers sink to the bottom of the success ladder in academic as well as professional life. Across a wide range of important occupations, givers appear at a disadvantage; they make others better off but sacrifice their own success in the process. The takers seem to surge ahead of the givers because they concentrate on fulfilling their personal agenda ahead of others. The matchers are like whistle-blowers, they keep a watch over takers so that they don't exploit other people. So, if givers are most likely to land at the bottom of the success ladder, who's at the top— takers or matchers? Neither. When Grant took another look at the data, he discovered a surprising pattern: It is the givers, again, who rise to the top of the success ladder. The takers and matchers stagnate in the middle. My own research shows that givers grow to the top by creating social capital. Social capital multiplied by their intellectual capital becomes their reputation capital. It is their reputation as large-hearted people that propels givers right to the top in the long run. Grant's research tells us that being a giver may not be good for a 100 metres dash, but it is valuable in a marathon.

If you wish to take your first firm steps towards happiness, move from your self-centred to the other-centred universe. Think of a few things you can do where you can put the best interest of others ahead of your own. The Dalai Lama gives you a solid spiritual reason to be other-centred. He advises people to cultivate the understanding that the self is not really an independently existing entity. He urges us to begin to view our self instead, in terms of its dependent relation to others. Although it is difficult to say that merely reflecting on this will produce profound happiness, it will at least have some effect. Your mind will be more open. Something will begin to change within you. Therefore, even in the immediate term, there is definitely a positive and beneficial effect in moving from self-centeredness to other-centeredness, from belief in self-existence to belief in dependent origination.

What do you think is the opposite of happiness? No, it is not sadness. To be sad and happy are like the trough and crest of the wave called life. They come together like winter and spring, rain and sunshine, shade and light. The opposite of happiness is selfishness. When we live in a self-centred rather than the other-centred universe, our life force shrinks like a rain-starved river. When we share our abundance with others, the same life force grows and makes us happy. Think of someone who wins a lottery yet has no one to share his fortune with. Do you think he will be a happy man?

Next time, when you buy two scoops of your favourite ice cream from a confectionary, just look around to see if you can find an undernourished boy who works 14 hours a day in a nearby tea stall. If you wish, just share one scoop of your ice cream with him. Chances are your experiment in being a giver will result in a broader smile and slimmer hips!

LEADERSHIP ROLE: FOSTERING UNITY IN DIVERSITY

Constant respect for people and uncompromising integrity are the two prerequisites for managing diversity in any organization, anywhere. Respect for people is not a cosmetic courtesy. It is not the proverbial, 'When in Rome, do as the Romans do.' This respect means 're-spect'. The syllable 'spect' has the same root as 'spectacle'; 'spect' means to see. Re-spect, therefore, means to re-view or to see again. Genuine respect only comes from the will to see a person not as a nodding acquaintance but as someone from whom we can learn, someone who is worthy of a second look. Respect is an attitudinal issue; it changes our attitude towards our co-workers and our neighbours. This kind of attitudinal change brings about greater harmony and promotes diversity. Uncompromising integrity, which is a basic value for understanding and promoting diversity, comes from self-respect. Only when we learn to respect ourselves can we learn to respect others. The self and the other are connected by a common value—the value of humanness. At a more profound level, this common ground exists in our spiritual unity.

The Dalai Lama, talking about his own realization about the interconnected reality of the self and the other, said, 'In fact, self and other are relative, like this side of the mountain and that side of the mountain. From my perspective, I am self and you are other, but from your perspective, you are self and I am other' (Lama et al. 1995).

Unity in diversity is the secret of nature's organization. With this principle, nature keeps its various constituents in a state of dynamic equilibrium. In the organization of an ecosystem, the soil, the plants, the insects and the animals exist as a rich diversity. Yet they are united in an interrelationship not only with each other but also with the system as a whole. The balance of unity in diversity is very dynamic. Each species in this ecosystem is evolving towards unity. This evolution is what we know as love.

It is not enough for leaders, simply, to recognize intellectually that a certain unity exists amidst the diversity in their organizations. Leaders must feel this unity in their blood and in their bones. This feeling comes from *ekatmanubhuti*, a Sanskrit, classical-Indian expression meaning unity of spirit. In this state of feeling, leaders recognize that unity in diversity is the deep-seated democracy that underlies nature's organization. They then begin to value relationships within the organization as relationships of feeling as well as relationships of function. Leadership becomes an embodiment of *ekatmanubhuti*, unity of spirit, which is the ultimate human value.

HOW TO CHANGE

The only way to grow is by changing our mind. The only way to change our mind is to learn. The best way to learn is to do something we have not done before.

Taking on a new role means that you have to give up on the comforts of the old role. This requires dealing with resistance to change. The first point of resistance is felt in our brain chemistry. Old ways, stagnant habituations of comfort, die-hard habits—all these are entrenched in our neural architecture. It is easier to pull a rabbit out of a hat rather than a habit out of a rut.

I would suggest that my friends in professional life should seriously consider this: If you have been doing the same job for two years, scrutinize your work carefully to see if you are learning anything new. If you are doing it for four years, look at your work with caution and see if you are satisfactorily underperforming. In case you are doing the same work for eight years, you are either a moron or a master! After 10 years, you must learn to move on, unless you have certified yourself as an enlightened being.

Two monks met for a meditation break. 'Where are you brother?' asks the younger monk.

'I am in that place where nothing ever changes,' comes the reply from the old monk.

'But I thought everything in this world was always changing,' argued the young monk.

'Yes, that never changes either,' said the old monk laughing uncontrollably.

No human being grows without a change of mind. Yet it is easier to teach a zebra some algebra than to change your made-up mind. The made-up mind is like the shell of an egg. Unless the shell is cracked open, life within it stagnates and dies. Life within us forces the mind to open up from time to time. The mind opens up to reality when an unexpected event occurs such as an unlikely promotion or the untimely death of a loved one. My thumb rule is—the unexpected breaks the shell of the made-up mind. Therefore, the unexpected gives us a taste of reality beyond the projections of the made-up mind. Like an umbrella, the mind functions best when it is open to facing changing environmental conditions.

Change of mind happens as we change the trajectory of thoughts. Mind is nothing but an accumulation of a pattern of thoughts and emotions. When this pattern is repeated time and again, the mind becomes as hard as the shell of an egg. Some effort is needed to break the shell. The right effort can come following these three steps:

1. Think of your memory as a Rewind button of your mind.
2. Think of your will as the Stop button
3. Think of your action as the Play button.

You cannot change your mind by rewinding old thoughts. You cannot use your will to stop the non-stop flow of thoughts from the past to the future. All you can do is play with a new set of actions that you have not performed before. If you do not play with new action choices, you will not be anyone different.

IDENTITY AND THE DEEP ROOTS OF CHANGE

In a human organization, change takes place on the enduring foundation of human identity. As human beings, we accept change that enhances our sense of well-being and our identity. Any change that threatens our basic identity is resisted. That is the law of human nature.

The identity of an organization, like that of a nation, is composed of the collective identities of its people and their beliefs, practices and values. Systems can be acted on and structures can be manipulated, but a collective identity is, almost, impossible to erase.

Leaders, as agents of change, need to explore the roots of this heritage right from the founding ethos and history of the organization. Leaders need to ask, 'What is that spirit of enterprise that has brought the organization into being in the first place?' For those of us in leadership positions who are still sceptical about comprehending our past for understanding the future of our present, I can do no better than quote these wonderful lines from Bertrand Russell's book, *The Scientific Outlook*: 'Men in the past were often parochial in space, but the dominant men of our age are parochial in time. They feel for the past a contempt that it does not deserve, and for the present a respect that it deserves still less' (Russell 1931).

12

LOVE

Do not waste time bothering whether you 'love' your neighbour; act as if you did.

—C. S. Lewis

LEADERSHIP: LOVE IN ACTION

Bill George, the former CEO of Medtronic, is an example of a corporate leader who subscribes to this leadership philosophy. Bill finds inspiration in the words of Kahlil Gibran, 'Work is love made visible.' One hears in Bill's voice the conviction of a person who has experienced the energy of love in his leadership work at Medtronic. At a presentation to business school students, Bill quoted the entire passage from Gibran as though he were saying an earnest prayer:

> Work is love made visible. And if you cannot work with love but only with distaste, it is better that you should leave your work and sit at the gate of the temple and take alms of those who work with joy. (Gibran 1970)

Bill completely identifies with the mission of Medtronic, which is 'to help people lead fuller lives'. He said, 'We restore people to the fullness of life. That mission is easy for me to identify with.'

Love in the context of work is not a noun but a verb. Love is not simply recognizing the objective value of a given work. Rather, it is the process of creating value in any work we do.

In our psychological universe, love generates our social and parental instincts, builds friendships, unites lovers and creates an affinity between people in organizations. In the larger spiritual realm, love raises the human organism beyond the pursuit of physical and social needs towards a greater integration with the cosmos.

Conscious leaders are aware of love in action. They know that if work is creation, then love is the creative impulse behind it. These leaders trace the mysterious source of love not in the objective arena of action but within their own hearts. Love is not a mere feeling present on the surface of experience; it has to be traced to the depths of one's being and to the ultimate source of one's great actions.

In my growing-up years in India, the person from whom I had learned all about love was my own grandmother. For her, love meant the joy of letting go! Her favourite fruit was the royal mango. Yet I had never seen her eat a single mango. She would slice delicate crimson-green mangoes with surgical precision for her visitors. She would watch with indulgent grace as gluttonous guests slurped trickling yellow juices off their fingers. Yet she would not eat a single mango herself. One day I asked her, 'Why?' She blushed like a ripe Alfonso and sporting her toothless smile said, 'My husband, when he was alive, loved to eat mangoes more than anything else. When he died, I decided to give up the fruit that I could not share with him.'

Long years of silence stretched between my grandmother's mellowed wisdom and my raw, green understanding.

I learned, over the years, that attachment can, sometimes, blind you to the greater dimension of love. Letting go was not about losing but about voluntarily moving aside from the usual addictive appetites to taste the experience of freedom and joy. It is better to sometimes lose in love rather than triumph. You know why? Losing gives you a measure of your attachment to the temporary and the transient.

NATURE OF LOVE: THREE HABITS OF THE HEART

The heart has been acknowledged by the great masters of antiquity as a potential source of wisdom and intelligence. The sacred traditions held that a pure heart was the foundation for purity and clarity of perception.

First of all, we associate the heart with desire, as in the statement, 'I ate to my heart's content.' Desire is the first stirring of life in the biological universe; it is the primary impulse for living. When the energy of desire works purely at the physical level, it is regulated by a control mechanism built into our physical nature. Our desire for water is quenched as soon as the body's thirst is met. But the problem arises when desire overshoots the limit of the physical and trespasses on the mental world. This happens because the undigested physical experience leaves its residue on the mind in the form of memory. It is the memory of unfulfilled pleasurable sensation that gives birth to desire.

When our desire for a pleasant experience turns into a dysfunctional response of habit, we can conclude that our ardour has truly turned into an addiction. Even our routine action can turn into addiction when we are unable to let go of our mental engagement with work in which we are not physically engaged any longer.

Conscious leaders act from the core of their hearts. Their desire for action is channelled entirely into the immediate context of the present. They act in the here and now with great love. In this way, they master desire rather than allow themselves to be mastered by it. If this action is total and instantaneous, it does not spill over into other useless activity and nervous agitation. It is then that the leader can claim to have cultivated the first habit of the heart—to channel the energy of desire along the path of the desirable.

Another way in which the heart expresses itself is through passion. Passion is a sustained form of desire for something. When someone says, 'I have a passion for music', they are expressing their long-term love for music. Passion is a quality of the heart.

In passion, the heart of the leader rises from the flickering impulse of egocentric desire towards a steady flame of aspiration.

The second habit of the heart is, therefore, to guide the flame of passion towards compassion. In leadership, compassion is the culmination of the leader's passion. In being compassionate, leaders develop integral bonds of fellowship with their followers.

The third habit of the heart is that it sees everything in its entirety and not in parts unlike the intellect of a human being that computes form and phenomenon by means of the twin processes of fragmentation and analysis.

Wholeness is the result of an experience of unity within the self. When we are united within ourselves, we can see life in a multiplicity of dimensions. In wholeness, we do not see the mere surface of reality but probe its very depths. Wholeness is an experience; it is a feeling. It is returning to the centre of our being. In the words of Lord Byron:

KARMA SUTRAS

> I live not in myself, but I become
>
> Portion of that around me: and to me
>
> High mountains are a feeling....

—Lord Byron, *Childe Harold's Pilgrimage*, canto III, 1816

In wholeness, we have a chance to experience the richness and dynamism of life. Corporate leaders who are directly in touch with their subordinates and who shake hands with them once in a while are experiencing wholeness. If the same leader were to be acquainted with their subordinates through their biographical data in computer printouts, they would experience only a fragment and not the whole person. Albert Einstein was describing the rare experience of wholeness when he said that small is the number of them that see with their own eyes and feel with their own hearts.

FROM HIGH-TECH TO HIGH-TOUCH LEADERSHIP

The secret of high-touch leadership is simply this: paying attention to and lending your heart to the details. In contemporary leadership, there is a declining market for lofty speeches and noble thoughts. All that followers want to see in their leaders is a life lived in details, according to stated principles. The followers' perceptions of their leaders are based not on the halos around the latter but on the attention paid by the leaders to the infinitesimal details of day-to-day living.

Earl Bakken of Medtronic understands the importance of high-touch leadership as he travels the world from Minneapolis to Tokyo, meeting each of his 9,000 employees in small groups of 15–20 people at a time. The employees value their leader's gift of touch. Relationships endure in Medtronic as a result of this.

The dimensions of the sense of touch go beyond the physical and psychological planes. Most ancient civilizations were aware of the spiritual aspect of touch. In India, the essential spiritual nature of touch was known as *sparsa tattva*. Spiritual wisdom from the master to the disciple was sometimes communicated through *sparsa* or touch.

Gandhi understood the importance of high-touch leadership in a human organization. He said, 'Work with the hands is the apprenticeship of honesty. May the work of your hands be a sign of gratitude and reverence to the human condition.' Great leaders like Gandhi think of their hands not only as instruments of the body and the mind but also as spiritual partners. Whether it is a handshake or a namaste, the intro-ductory, face-to-face meeting between two human beings often involves the use of hands. Both are profound gestures that build bridges of understanding between people.

Leaders, in our highly technological society, have tended to keep in touch with reality through impersonal push-button systems of communication. Relationships built through high-tech methods such as faxes and e-mail have their advantages, of course, because they standardize and economize on the cost and time of communication. But in this quest for stan-dardization of communication procedures, leaders miss out on the uniqueness of old-fashioned human touch. William Hauser, head of the technical department at AT&T for several years, told me how he felt the loss of human contact with the advent of e-mail. An old-timer with AT&T, Hauser has experi-enced how people come together less and less in their offices and how they prefer e-mailing or teleconferencing from their

KARMA SUTRAS

homes. This, he said, has resulted in the loss of value of the human touch in the organization.

LEADERSHIP AND INTIMACY: THE FEMININE CONSCIOUSNESS

An organization is a web of intimate relations. The organization is greater than the sum of its constituent parts not because the parts are merely added on but because they are related. The organization, as a whole, is a relational pattern that remains even when individual members come and go. The leaves of a tree grow and die every season, but the dynamic pattern of the whole tree remains.

Intimacy is a state of awareness. It is not simply physical proximity. Two people can be intimate even when they are thinking on the same wavelength. It requires a special quality of consciousness to be truly intimate. I would like to describe this special quality as 'receptivity'.

Receptivity nurtures the spirit of accommodation. It is the ability to push the limits of our capacity to absorb and accept reality. It is the polar opposite of power and aggression. It comes not from the love of power but the power of love. It empowers one in spirit. Even Napoleon Bonaparte acknowledged the power of the spirit over the power of force in the last days of his life. He said, 'Do you know what astonished me the most in the world? The inability of force to create anything. In the long run, the sword is always defeated by the spirit.'

The feminine consciousness is truly receptive. It accepts, tolerates and transforms. It embraces the aggressive impulse of the outgoing masculine energy and transforms it into a higher order of creativity. Jesus Christ on the cross is the highest embodiment of the feminine power of tolerance over the masculine power of brute force. Gandhi used the soft but unyielding force of non-violence to overcome aggression.

Leadership requires the capacity to absorb the conflicting energies of group members. This shock-absorbing mechanism makes it possible for leaders to be a confluence of diverse energies. By embodying the receptive quality of feminine consciousness, leaders consolidate the dissipative energies of their organizations for greater effectiveness.

All organizations develop themselves through two broad phases. The first is the phase of conquest, and the second is the phase of consolidation. Conquest represents the expansion of energy by means of building more capacity, capturing new markets, increasing human power, innovating technology, creating new products and raising more capital. Consolidation represents conservation of energy by developing core competencies, retraining the existing workers, improving the quality of existing products and increasing capacity utilization.

Some cultures have, in the course of their evolutionary history, created the identity of the feminine in terms of greater resilience and receptivity. In a culture like that of India, highly qualified women assuming leadership positions in all spheres of society acknowledge this social-historical factor in determining their leadership quality.

In traditional societies like that of India, in which a woman's household work has no cash value, there is increasing pressure on women to work in offices and then come home to perform what may be called, in factory parlance, the second shift. This has brought about a remarkable shift in Indian women's perspective on leadership. These women lead not only by being resourceful at home but also by assuming new responsibilities at the office. Responsibility is a newly discovered leadership trait among Indian women. It was not as if women were not responsible at home, but this responsibility was hitherto unrecognized as something that has a real value.

✳13✳

NATURE'S MANUSCRIPT

The butterfly counts not months but moments, and has time enough.

—Rabindranath Tagore

CONSCIOUSNESS IN NATURE

It was a practice among rulers in ancient India to retreat into the forest to renew their perspective on worldly matters. In the quietude of the forest, they could ponder, reflect and launch themselves on a journey of self-discovery. This retreat was an important phase in the life of a householder and was known in ancient times as *vanaprastha* or the 'phase of the forest'. The ancient masters believed that there was consciousness in the hidden depths of nature, and that this consciousness was accessible to a human being who could enter into intimate communion with nature.

In the unheard language of nature, there is absolute unity of sound and meaning. There is a purity of expression in the sound of the forest that cannot be found in the misleading voices of concrete corporate jungles. All of nature is, in fact, an effusion of unheard language. Only human beings limit this flow of sound through social conditioning. If we have keen ears, we can hear the timeless vibrations of truth in the rustle of the leaves, in the buzzing of the bees and in the rippling waters of a river. Nature articulates the vibratory structure of all forms of this earth within the unitary stream of consciousness. The

Sanskrit word *mantra* best describes the language of conscious nature.

The language of *mantra* can be coherently understood in terms of its prime root meanings. These roots do not have narrow, rigid meanings; they generally are intelligent vibrations of sound that help create meaning and give form to the formless.

A leader need not be a romantic visionary to appreciate the marvellous precision and harmony in nature's management. It is a harmony born out of a quest for truth and beauty, a search for symbiosis and an unerring instinct for unity in diversity.

A conscious leader realizes that nature never stands up like an egotistic demon and proclaims, 'I am the monarch of all I survey.' Even the tallest tree recognizes its debt to the soil with humility. The elements of nature hardly ever exploit one another as passive resources. They do not dominate or plunder each other in self-seeking madness. All of nature is conscious of the fact that in the welfare of all is the welfare of one.

THREE LAWS OF LEADING CONSCIOUSLY

When we come out of the complex maze of corporate life to look at the vast expanse of nature, we are struck by the stark simplicity of the natural world. This simplicity is neither monotonous nor monochromatic. There is a tremendous diversity of colour and sound in nature's organization. Yet there is a discernible effortlessness with which nature manoeuvres this diversity of form and phenomena into a harmonious whole.

A spider's web is an example of the marvellous organization found in nature. The web starts as a simple Y-shaped structure made from the secretion of the spider. The spider spins around this basic structure to produce a web of increasing subtlety and complexity. There is tremendous flexibility and adaptability in the spider's organization. Leadership in nature's organization emerges from a consciousness that can comprehend the whole. To be able to comprehend the whole, this consciousness has to be aware of the relationship between things and their contexts and not merely between the things themselves.

The greatest challenge that faces leaders today is to strike a balance between the sustenance of the entire context of an organization while nurturing individual identities within it. The environmental and ethical concerns of modern organizations point towards the same dilemma. I believe that only nature has an answer to this riddle of the relation between the parts and the whole. For this, we need to look at the three laws of conscious leadership, which I have drawn from nature's manuscript. These laws are as follows:

1. The law of complete concentration
2. The law of detached awareness
3. The law of transcendence

The first of these laws is the 'law of complete concentration'. Concentration enables nature to achieve a purity of purpose. This purity comes from the arrangement of the disorganized elements of nature into one coherent whole. A solution of saltwater left to itself exhibits this natural phenomenon. In the solution, the dissolved components of the salt tend to concentrate into salt crystals, which is nothing but pure salt.

The second law of conscious leadership is the 'law of detached awareness'. This seems like a paradoxical statement: How can one be aware of something and yet remain detached? Whenever I am asked to explain this point in my leadership workshops, I use an analogy taught to me by my teacher.

'Imagine the hand of a mother holding on to the hand of a one-year-old who has just learned to walk,' I say. 'The mother has to soften her grip enough to enable the child to walk freely. But she has to hold on firmly enough to ensure that the child does not lose balance.' When we concentrate too hard on something or some thought, we tend to put up an energy wall of resistance against total awareness. For example, when we struggle to listen to an announcement in a busy subway train, we try hard to tune out other noises. In making this effort, we lose some energy in building up resistance to what we consider undesirable noise. But those who have learned the discipline of concentrating their thoughts on a thing or an idea for a considerable period of time do not feel the need to resist anything from invading their awareness.

The 'law of transcendence' automatically follows the law of detached awareness. A scientist looking for evidence of truth under a microscope is a detached observer. The keener their observation, the closer they come to the truth behind the observed form or phenomenon. A time comes when the observation is so pure that the scientist eventually zeroes in on the truth. In this act, the observer, the thing being observed and the process of observation are united in one experience. This is the experience of transcendence.

BREATH: THE BRIDGE TO TRANSCENDENCE

Our breath is a bridge to our transcendental reality. Breathing is much more than the physiologic act known as respiration. It is a subtle process that links us with our vast, limitless existence. In simple words, our breathing makes us really and truly existential. With every inhalation, we breathe in several million atoms of the universe.

Watch what happens to your breathing when you are angry. Your breath becomes more and more shallow, your chest heaves and your nostrils flare to accommodate as much air as possible. As the normal pattern of your breathing is disrupted, you are thrown off balance, both mentally and physiologically. All our emotional experiences are intimately linked with the way we breathe. Proper management of breathing constitutes the fine art of living in harmony with existence.

The simplest of breathing exercises can be practised through breathing in and breathing out with awareness. While you breathe out, say to yourself, 'With each out-breath, I go out to the world.' And while you breathe in, tell yourself, 'With each in-breath, I come back to myself.' This rhythm of going out and coming in is one of the most fundamental rhythms of life.

The ancient Indian masters recognized that *prana*, or vital breath, is the basic unit of energy that perpetuates life. According to them, this fundamental energy expresses itself in five primary life currents. These are *prana* (outgoing breath), *apana* (incoming breath), *vyana* (retained breath), *udana* (ascending breath) and *samana* (equalizing breath). *Pranayama* is the ancient discipline of regulating these life currents for effective living.

By inhabiting our gross body alone, we live in a partial and fragmented world. Here, we are like the owner of a multi-storied mansion who lives on only one floor of the house. The connecting link between the gross body and the subtle body or the mental body is being discovered today in medical research. The ancients knew several thousand years ago about the existence of the integral body–mind–consciousness axis that constitutes the human being. More importantly, they knew that the way to gain access to the multidimensional nature of our being is through conscious breathing.

STEP 1: EXPERIENCING THE LAW OF COMPLETE CONCENTRATION

Sit comfortably on a chair with your feet placed firmly on the floor. Do not assume either a sloppy or a stiff posture. Balance yourself on the chair comfortably enough so that you can stay in that position for 10–15 minutes. It helps if the backbone, neck and head are aligned properly as you sit.

Close your eyes and remain alert to your body's functioning. Slowly focus your attention on your breathing. With your eyes closed, be fully aware as you breathe in and breathe out. Remain attentive for not more than a couple of seconds to the silent gap between inhaling and exhaling. Do not hold your breath at any point.

As you breathe consciously and deeply for about 15 times, you will experience a wonderful thing. Your mind will, automatically, become concentrated and your breathing will assume a soothing rhythm. This is the experience of the law of complete concentration.

STEP 2: EXPERIENCING THE LAW OF DETACHED AWARENESS

Already concentrated in body and mind through conscious breathing, with your eyes closed, shift your attention from your breathing to your thoughts. This time do not concentrate. Just be alert to the steady stream of thoughts in your brain space. You may visualize your thoughts passing by like busy traffic on a road or, better still, like clouds in a sky. Do not become attached to your thoughts; just be a witness to them. Look for the gap between your thoughts. Never mind if your attention strays; just bring it back with gentle persuasion. Remind yourself that you are not your thoughts; you are only watching them.

Your thoughts will slowly diminish in number. As you detach yourself more and more from your thoughts, you will grow in awareness. This awareness is what was described earlier as *sakshi*. At this stage, your breathing automatically becomes slower and you are ready to experience transcendence.

STEP 3: EXPERIENCING THE LAW OF TRANSCENDENCE

With your eyes closed, take your awareness farther up to the top of your head. Do not concentrate. Completely relax your attention. Visualize that you are gently opening up at the top of your head, just as the petals of a flower unfold one by one to receive sunlight. This opening up is only a visual metaphor to enable your psychosomatic structure to experience a progressive sense of transcendence. As you visualize the opening of a flower and experience its fragrance as it is released into the air, you are psychologically transported to a realm of pure light and consciousness. There is no concentration here, no urge to attach or detach; it is an experiment in letting go.

NATURE'S WORK: INERTIA, DYNAMISM AND AWARENESS

Nature's work is an exquisite synthesis of inertia, dynamism and awareness. These are the three fundamental modes of expression in nature. These three processes can be seen at work in both the physical and psychological universe. Inertia, the first state, is the state of passivity; it is the seed form of physical or psychological action.

Dynamism, the second process, is the movement from non-action to action and from passivity to passion. It is the stage of the growth and evolution of form and phenomenon. Awareness, the third process, represents another dimension of evolution—the evolution of consciousness.

The mineral world represents inertia. Rocks remain the same for millions of years; the change in them is too slow to be detected with our physical senses. The plant kingdom represents a gradual movement from inertia to dynamism.

Awareness, the third quality of nature, is something that is largely dormant in plants and is present in a very rudimentary stage in the animal kingdom. In human beings, we see the first real evidence of self-awareness. The power of conscious thought and action in the human universe comes from this self-awareness. To be completely self-aware is the highest expression of human evolution.

How does dynamism evolve into the quality of awareness? This is one of the most remarkable secrets of nature. The ancient masters of India understood that nature, including human nature, evolves along two paradoxical paths. One is the path of *pravritti*, in which nature exteriorizes its energy and bursts out into a riot of forms and shapes and colours. In the psychological universe of human beings, *pravritti* carves out the path of desire and ambition. The second path of nature is the way of *nivritti*. It is the interiorized and inward-looking energy in nature. On this path, nature hibernates, arrests growth and pulls inward the energy that would otherwise be frittered away in outward expression.

In nature, the principle and the process of leadership work together. The process is the visible relation between various aspects of nature, and the principle is the underlying law that keeps these processes in order.

A conscious leader makes creative use of the principles as well as the processes of inertia, dynamism and awareness. Rajat Gupta, the first non-American CEO of McKinsey & Company, allows some problems to remain undecided because he is conscious that a certain amount of inertia is more useful

KARMA SUTRAS

in solving a problem than premature and aggressive action. He said, 'I tend to let things sort themselves out. Nine problems out of ten go away if you don't address them. You have to deal with the tenth. I often don't address things until I have to.'

A DAY IN YOUR LIFE

Nothing defines you more than a day in your life! In one way, a day is like a perpetual prison. In the course of a day, we enter into a jail of our habituation. Just consider your typical day: brushing your teeth, rushing through a shower, browsing a newspaper, brewing coffee, chewing breakfast, a comatose commute to your place of work, an encounter with your boss, shuffling papers, ruffling tempers, commuting back home, watching a soap and cuddling a pet before finally hitting the bed. Incidentally, in this time prison of your own making, you are both the jailor and the jailed.

Now, consider another day that you chose for yourself: Getting up a good half hour before you usually do; brushing your teeth with the wrong hand; reading a section of the newspaper you usually don't; skipping coffee for a beverage that you used to have as a kid; making your own breakfast; doing a few more stretches; walking to work; presenting your boss a book that he might read; deciding that you will not judge anybody in the office today; buying some yellow roses on your way back home; coming out to your balcony to watch the sunset; taking a musical bath with your favourite instrumental music turned on; viewing television with the sound muted; and reading yourself to sleep with an inspiring storybook.

A day can burn or bore you out. When you drag yourself through the rut of a routine life, you are likely to douse the flame of your enthusiasm. Routine is important; rotting is not. When was the last time that you learnt something for the first time? I know a medical doctor who fell in love and danced salsa for the first time when he was nearly 70 years old! Alongside the rigour of routine, you require a ritual of renewal. Why? If you look around in nature, you will see that life is never linear. A burst of activity in nature is always followed by a bout of relaxation. Life in nature is circular: changing seasons, waxing and waning of the moon, shifting constellation of stars—all of these point towards the urge for renewal and rejuvenation.

In human beings, energy moves in non-linear ways. Our attention is the primary source of our energy. You can hold your attention intensely on a subject for about 90 minutes or so. After that, your attention is likely to flag. Desire is another source of energy. Whatever we deeply desire will energize us to pursue the object of our desire. However, this pursuit has to be punctuated with necessary diversion. Can you kiss someone for hours without wanting to do anything else, however desirable that kiss may be? Moderation is critical to the management of human energy. Moderation involves slowing down, pacing ourselves to be in sync with the rhythms of our energy.

Our emotions are deep sources of our energy. If you observe the energy associated with your emotions, you will realize that there is waxing and waning in the movement of emotions. How long, at a stretch, can you feel anger or affection for someone? An hour? Two hours? You will discover that the emotions of anger and affection come and go like day and night. Emotions are energy bubbles in motion. You have to be an observer of the course of your emotion in a whole day. In the observatory that is located inside you, you will see a constellation of emotions. You will discover that anger, fear, happiness, lust, jealousy—all these emotions emerge in a pattern in the course of a day.

KARMA SUTRAS

Take all the 15 odd hours of waking time in the course of a single day. Divide those 15 hours into your typical energy chunks! You will find out that you feel deeply energized during some parts of the day and thoroughly depleted of energy and enthusiasm during the rest. How do you live the rest of your day like the best of your day? Just think of this—today is the first and last day of the rest of your life. You have been given the gift of this day. How will you express your gratitude to the giver? You are not fully certain that you will wake up alive inside the same room that you will go to bed in. Not everyone in our world will wake up tomorrow on this beautiful earth. With this realization, how will you choose to live today? Just think of it before you seize the day!

NATURE'S CYCLE: A TRYST WITH TIME

Nature is a perfect example of the art of waiting. It takes the evolutionary impulse of nature's several thousand years to perfect the shape of a single flower. When we look at natural processes, we realize that there is a certain wisdom implicit in the paradox: Faster is slower.

There is conscious energy found in patience that provides an impetus towards right action at the right time. Nature demonstrates this day after day.

Only human beings seem to have problems in managing time. No other species on earth, apparently, suffers from this problem, which is peculiar to our industrial civilization. The problem of time appears to have emerged with the invention of the clock.

In nature, time is never linear; it is cyclical. The laws of nature clearly tell us that time is not irreversible. We see the reversal of time in our psychological universe in the form of the memory of past events. From the memory of physical nature, seasons come back year after year, crops grow, the sun rises and sets, and the planets go round and round in their orbits.

In defiance of the modern perception of time as a chronologic journey, it may be said that time is not a one-way public thoroughfare; it is also a private apartment. I am talking here about personal time. In the context of space, what we see depends on where we sit. In the context of time, our perspective on time influences how we process time in our consciousness. When our awareness has a chance to expand in time, as when we are in love, time moves at a dizzying speed. When our awareness is constricted in a certain time, as when we are doing an unpleasant chore, time seems to stand still, like a burden on our backs.

Apart from chronological time, which is unidirectional, there is also biological and psychological time, which is non-linear and multidimensional. Chronological time emerges from the fragmentation of time into the past, present and future. In this kind of time, the present is always referred to in terms of the past or the future. It is as if the present is non-existent. A look at the movement of the hands of a mechanical clock reveals that this movement is not smooth but jerky. The hands jump from the past to the future, bypassing the moment. This linear movement of chronological time, in fits and starts, speeds up our psychological clock. As a result, we are never present in the moment and are forever present in the fictitious past or the imaginary future.

Nature lives in a simultaneous world of time and timelessness. All changes in the natural world belong to time.

Conscious leaders work in time but live in the world of the timeless. Their lives serve as glorious links between their predecessors and the unborn generations of tomorrow. The actions of conscious leaders are prompted not so much by the pressing needs of their own survival but by the higher aspiration of life to perpetuate itself.

NATURE'S MANUSCRIPT: MEDITATIONS FOR LEADERS

THE FREEDOM OF THE SKY

A tired man returning home after a gruelling day's work encounters a bleak, soulless city. The sun has slipped behind the skyscrapers. Streetlights wink eerily through the heavy smog. The din of traffic drowns out the call of a bird perched on an electric wire. The man feels the agony of having to make a living in this cage-like city. He looks heavenward for relief only to discover that even the sky has been blotted out by giant billboards.

Yet the sky remains for many of us a constant reminder that we are, essentially, free beings and dwellers of the infinite. The endless blue we see above us defies the geometry of the cityscape. The sky is an open invitation to us to experience the freedom of the formless.

Freedom is a state of consciousness. It does not lie outside us. Rather, our search for freedom is an inward quest, a journey within to liberate ourselves from our self-created prisons. Stone walls, the poet Lovelace said, do not make a prison; our mental blocks do. The iron bars of our fears and prejudices hold us in psychological bondage. They do not allow us to taste the freedom that is our birth right. The Upanishads say that the prime goal of human beings is the attainment of freedom or *moksha*. The Buddhists call this nirvana or the extinction of bondage.

Tibetan lamas often teach their disciples to meditate on the sky. The disciples are advised to lie flat on their backs, preferably in the open, to get a clear view of the sky. Alternatively, they are advised to look up to the sky while standing or sitting in a comfortable position. One has to make sure that the line of vision is not obstructed by other objects. As one contemplates the vast blue of the sky, one's consciousness expands progressively.

THE MESSAGE OF THE MOUNTAINS

Mountains teach us the art of detachment. They inspire us to transcend the mundane, increase in strength and aspire to all that is the highest and purest in the world. The mountain listens silently to the magnificent music of the wind as it sweeps across its rocky face.

There is a mountain in our psyche that corresponds to that in physical nature; the only difference between them is a difference in scale and perspective.

One has to abandon many creature comforts when climbing a mountain. In renouncing our attachment to these comforts of the plains, we come in touch with a consciousness of the sacred. Mount Kailash in India, Mount Fuji in Japan, the T'ai Shan in China—all have been revered as sacred places by some of the world's most enduring civilizations.

In the earth-defying silence of the mountain, we encounter a vertical pull of a higher state of consciousness. The physical altitude triggers a psychic journey into a higher realm of awareness. Those of us who have meditated deeply on the mountain intuitively know this. Mountain climbing is not only a rigorous physical act but also a demanding mental, psychological and spiritual act. A climber learns great lessons about the importance of reaching goals in the process of climbing.

LESSONS FROM A GARDEN

If you spend some time in a Japanese garden, you will see a miniature landscape of the human mind. You may call it a mindscape. You will see an assortment of foliage—flowers, bushes, shrubs, trees—the names of which you may not know. I have often found a garden's fascinating contours similar to the inner world of a human being.

The solid rocks are like the fortresses of values that are deeply entrenched in the heart and that gives us a sense of stability in an ever-changing world. The running water, sparkling in the sun, is the clear stream of reason that winds its way through the dense mass of ignorance. The soft, moist soil is a fertile bed of emotion on which grow flowers of many colours and forms—the peaceful white lily, the bold red rose and the flamboyant chrysanthemum.

The wind leaves its impression on our senses just as it affects everything else in the garden. It caresses the silken flower petals, rustles through the dried leaves and inscribes its message on the sand.

As I sat reflecting on the beauty of the garden, a sudden insight came to me: If our mind is like a garden, then it must be the creation of a gardener, who is the master of this unique, little universe.

I conjectured that our own minds, like the garden, are perhaps a projection of a higher mind. Our minds are only a finite expression of a higher intelligence which conceived us.

Are we, therefore, not connected to this higher self just as the garden is integrally connected with the gardener? Perhaps, the only way to be in touch with the higher mind is to suspend the boundaries of our limited minds and to dissolve ourselves into the unlimited, as the garden outside and the garden inside merge in the mind of the gardener. A prayer came to my heart in the middle of all these thoughts:

Let me be just one song,

A universe of thought, feeling, and action.

Let me touch the entire world

Just as the sun's rays caress the darkest planet.

Let me be as humble as a blade of grass

And as tolerant as a tree,

Which gives shade even to the one

Who prepares to cut it down.

SELF-ORGANIZING UNIVERSE

We often talk about our self in the environment. I would like to modify that statement in light of my own experience. I would like to say that one's self *is* the environment. This claim might lead to a crisis of perception among those of us who are accustomed to defining the outer limit of the self as the beginning of the environment. If, however, we define our environment, not in terms of objects but, simply, as a set of relationships, it becomes clear that nothing can be part of our environment if it is not related to our self. Whatever is related to our self becomes a part of us.

We live not in a world of objects but a universe of relationships. Even so-called objects are not quite objects; they are relationships. The house in which we live is not an object; it is a relationship among brick, wood, sand, cement and the hand that built it. The car we drive is in a relationship among its various mechanical and electronic parts, the fuel and the driver. We ourselves are a bundle of relationships, forming a bridge between our ancestors and our descendants.

The unique dimension that makes a relational world viable is the process of self-organization. A caterpillar contains a set of relationships that can reorganize themselves and become a butterfly. A piece of coal is a relationship between several atoms of carbon. When this relationship changes, the same carbon atoms combine to form a diamond.

The universe of self-organization is finite in its expression and infinite in its principle. It is finite in the sense that it revolves around a specific identity from which the organization flows. The self-organizing corporation, however, goes beyond the products themselves in search of new relationships between products and people. The commercial identity of Sony was related to the business of manufacturing and selling tape recorders and headphones. Yet the power of self-organization within Sony led to the creation of a new product based on the relationship between a tape recorder and a headphone—the Walkman. Walkman was the beginning of a new relationship between Sony and its customers. The self-organizing capability of computer technology has led to the building of bridges or relationships between computers and communication, between computers and transportation, between computers and management, and so on.

Self-organization is the law of being of all sentient life in our universe. The ancient Indian masters realized this clearly when they went in search of what they described as dharma. Dharma is the emergent property of all living forms that enables them to relate to their environment. It is not apparent because it is inherent not in objects but in relationships.

Conscious leaders are not in search of power or knowledge. They are, simply, in search of the self. In this search, they realize that the root of all power and knowledge lies deep within the dharma of the self. The moment one discovers one's dharma, one also spontaneously discovers one's unique relationship with the world. One is, then, like a bird that with the first flutter of its wings discovers its relationship with the air. The leader's power to fly lies in this relationship.

Each one of us in leadership positions is asking the same question in different languages and different contexts. The question is: How can I be my very best? Many of us realize that we can be our very best when we are truly related to ourselves, to our own dharma. In that relationship alone can we find our relatedness to the world at large.

14

EPILOGUE: THE SACRED PATH OF LEADERSHIP

Only mediocrities rise to the top in a system that won't tolerate wave making.

—Lawrence J. Peter

VIRTUOUS REALITY: THE LEADERSHIP PILGRIMAGE

A pilgrimage is different from all other kinds of journeys. In a pilgrimage, the destination lies within us. The true pilgrimage is as much a journey in space and time as it is a journey in consciousness. Leadership is a pilgrimage of consciousness. Leaders, in all fields of endeavour, provide perspective and direction to their followers. They not only see life in the context of the actual but also view it from the vantage point of the possible.

To undertake a pilgrimage, we must first have faith in the destination. In this case, the ultimate destination, as I have already said, is the self. Faith is something that is best described by the expression 'virtuous reality'. It has its own kind of logic and its own reality. Otherwise, how can one explain the fact that the largest and the most enduring organizations of the world are all based on faith? It is the search for constant truths about ourselves that inspires us to move into the realm of faith. In faith, we obey our own essence.

The second requirement for this leadership pilgrimage is the right kind of discipline. One has to discover, through trial and error, the right effort that will enable one to negotiate and overcome the obstacles that arise in one's path.

The third requirement for the leadership pilgrimage is the presence of a master. A master is simply a presence. A master is like the light of the lamp in whose presence we acquire clarity and luminosity on our journey.

In these last few pages, I present brief profiles of six world leaders who have led us by the light of their consciousness. They represent a tradition of the search for the sacred. Their pilgrimages towards self-mastery were nothing but heroic. In the course of their journeys, they transformed themselves and millions of others. They organized the masses into enduring institutions. Buddha, Gandhi, Mother Teresa, Lao Tzu, Confucius and Vivekananda, all have left their indelible footprints on the sands of time and deeply influenced our civilization.

The real crisis that faces us today is the crisis of consciousness. Those of us who hold positions of power and privilege in business, politics, academics, sports, medicine and organized religion must wake up and address this crisis. Leading consciously is not an esoteric formula for personal salvation; it is an urgent and emergent need for our own survival as a civilization. The leaders of tomorrow are destined to fulfil the dreams of the leaders of yesterday like Buddha, Gandhi and Mother Teresa. The conscious leaders of the 21st century will, no doubt, draw on the legacy of our great masters.

BUDDHA

Buddha means 'the awakened one'. When people, puzzled by his identity, asked him, 'Who are you? Are you a man? Or a god? Or an angel?' Buddha said, 'I am just awake.' Buddha, who was born around 563 BC, abandoned his princely life to end human suffering. Buddhism was born as a religion of infinite compassion.

Buddha's message set on fire the entire Indian subcontinent and spread to China, Tibet, Japan and eventually to the entire world. Buddha's message was direct, simple and practical. He said, 'What have I explained? I have explained the cause of suffering, and the destruction of suffering, and the path that leads to the destruction of suffering. For this is useful' (Smith 1991).

Buddha's leadership was evident not only in the size of his following and the spread of his order but also in the perfection of his discipline. He discovered the 'middle path' of leadership, which was the path of perceptive wisdom between the extremes of austerity and indulgence. He demonstrated the virtue of intense self-effort and self-reliance. He said, 'Those who, relying upon themselves only, shall not look for assistance to anyone besides themselves, it is they who shall reach the topmost height' (Smith 1991). His last words to his favourite disciple, Ananda, were, 'Be lamps unto yourselves. Attach yourselves to no external means. Hold fast as a refuge to the Truth. Work out your own salvation with diligence' (Smith 1991).

GANDHI: MY LIFE IS MY MESSAGE

Gandhi's entire life was an experiment with truth. He said, 'Truth is my God. Non-violence is the means of realizing Him' (Radhakrishnan 1956). On the basis of these two principles alone, this unarmed messiah of non-violence took on the might of the British empire and gave freedom to his country. After Buddha, Gandhi was the greatest spiritual force in the world history. No leader can describe himself accurately; he can only reveal himself through his actions. This is true of Gandhi. When a journalist asked him for a message for the people of the United States, Gandhi said, 'My life is its own message' (Radhakrishnan 1956).

There was fundamental integrity between Gandhi's leadership theory and practice. His speech, thought and action demonstrated amazing synchronicity. Gandhi believed firmly in the trusteeship principle of leadership. For him, a leader was responsible for holding in trust—the power given to him by his followers. Any misuse of this power was for Gandhi a betrayal of trust. Albert Einstein, a contemporary of Gandhi, said about him:

> The moral influence which he has exercised upon thinking people throughout the civilized world may be far more durable than would appear likely in our present age, with its exaggeration of brute force.... We are fortunate and should be grateful that fate has bestowed upon us so luminous a contemporary—a beacon to the generations to come. (Radhakrishnan 1956)

MOTHER TERESA: SMALL WORK WITH GREAT LOVE

Mother Teresa is an example of a leader whose power of love triumphed over love of power. Abandoning her career as a school teacher, she responded to the inner call of serving the poorest of the poor in the slums of Calcutta. She founded the Missionaries of Charity, which provides care and service to destitute people across the globe. She was described by the secretary-general of the United Nations as 'the most powerful woman in the world'.

Her leadership was based on a simple philosophy: small work with great love. She said about her mission, 'Our vocation is not the work. The fidelity to humble works is our means to put our love into action.' A tireless crusader for the underprivileged of the world, she led countless people on the path of service and love. Responding to a question about what she felt when people called her a living saint, she said with her characteristic humility:

> You have to be holy in your position as you are, and I have to be holy in the position that God has put me. So it is nothing extraordinary to be holy. Holiness is not the luxury of the few. Holiness is a simple duty for you and for me. We have been created for that.

LAO TZU: THE TAO OF LEADERSHIP

'To lead people, walk behind them,' said Lao Tzu, China's most revered philosopher and sage (Tao Te Ching). Lao Tzu literally means 'lithe old master'. According to Chinese tradition, Lao Tzu was born about 604 BC. This legendary figure is said to have written *Tao Te Ching* (The Way and Its Power), which is the second most translated book in the world after the Bible.

Lao Tzu was a mystic who spent most of his time in quiet contemplation. His life was an embodiment of the eternal and invisible principle that governs the world. According to Lao Tzu, mastery comes from understanding and harmonizing one's life with *Tao*, which is the ineffable and spontaneous order of nature. Leadership, according to him, is a state of consciousness. In the words of Lao Tzu, effective leadership comes from self-awareness and self-conquest: 'He who knows other men is discerning; he who knows himself is intelligent.

He who overcomes others is strong; he who overcomes himself is mighty' (Chatterjee 2008, 53).

CONFUCIUS: THE MORAL LEADER

Confucius, who lived from 551 to 479 BC, was a philosopher, teacher, kingmaker and social reformer. At the age of 70, he said about himself,

> At fifteen I began to be seriously interested in study. At thirty I had formed my character. At fifty I knew the will of heaven. At sixty nothing that I heard disturbed me. At seventy I could let my thoughts wander without trespassing the moral law. (Smith 1991)

Confucius single-handedly crafted an ethical, socially oriented philosophy that dominated Chinese civilization for many centuries. From the *Analects*, which contains the conversations of Confucius, we get the distilled wisdom of the world's most influential teacher and humanist.

Confucius looked upon the leader as the perfect gentleman. He said that leaders were like 'gentlemen who never compete'. For him, leadership was not an outcome of brute force and competitive rivalry, but rather a spontaneous flowering of moral power. Confucius said, 'To find the central clue to our moral being which unites us to the universal order that indeed is the highest human achievement.'

SWAMI VIVEKANANDA: SERVANT LEADERSHIP

'Everyone can play the role of the master but it is very difficult to be a servant,' said Swami Vivekananda. He was known as the 'cyclonic monk', who at the age of 39 left the world a legacy of unflinching service and institution building. Vivekananda (1863–1902) was the first living example, for the West, of the wisdom and spirit of India. Dedicating himself to his master, Vivekananda founded the order of Ramakrishna Mission, which survives worldwide more than a 100 years after his death, as a testimonial to his sound leadership.

'One must be a servant of servants and must accommodate a thousand minds. There must not be a shade of jealousy or selfishness. Then you are a leader,' said Vivekananda about the qualities of servant leadership. He embodied all the three attributes of a servant leader: purity of purpose, perseverance of effort and passion for service.

BIBLIOGRAPHY

FOREWORD

Chatterjee, Debashis. 1998. Foreword to *Leading Consciously: A Pilgrimage toward Self-Mastery,* by Peter Senge, 11. New York, NY: Butterworth-Heinemann.

PREFACE

Chatterjee, Debashis. 2008. *Leadership Sutras: A Pilgrimage toward Self-Mastery.* New Delhi: Elsevier.

PART I

CHAPTER 1

Candescence. Business Practices during the Great Depression. http://candescence-strategy.com/wp-content/uploads/2015/05/depression.pdf (accessed 5 June 2020).

Devaney, Susan. 2020, 12 May. Jacinda Ardern's Latest Speech Shows What True Leadership Looks Like. *Vogue.* https://www.vogue.co.uk/news/article/jacinda-ardern-leadership-coronavirus (accessed on 5 June 2020).

Friedman, Uri. 2020. New Zealand's Prime Minister May Be the Most Effective Leader on the Planet. *The Atlantic.* https://www.theatlantic.com/politics/archive/2020/04/jacinda-ardern-new-zealand-leadership-coronavirus/610237/ (accessed on 5 June 2020)

Kerrissey, Michaela, and Amy Edmondson. 2020, 13 April. What Good Leadership Looks Like during This Pandemic. *Harvard Business Review Digital Articles,* 2–7.

Manhire, Toby. 2020, 6 April. 'Jacinda Ardern: "Very Little of What I Have Done Has Been Deliberate. It's Intuitive".' *Guardian.* https://www.theguardian.com/world/2019/apr/06/jacinda-ardern-intuitive-courage-new-zealand (accessed on 1 June 2020).

McLay, Charlotte. 2019, 10 April. 'New Zealand Passes Law Banning Most Semiautomatic Weapons, Weeks After Massacre.' *New York Times.* https://www.nytimes.com/2019/04/10/world/asia/new-zealand-guns-jacinda-ardern.html (accessed on 1 June 2020).

New York Times. 2020, 30 April. 'In a Crisis, True Leaders Stand Out.' https://www.nytimes.com/2020/04/30/opinion/coronavirus-leadership.html (accessed on 4 June 2020).

Woodward, Ian. 2020, 1 May. 'Jacinda Ardern and Andrew Cuomb Are Crisis Comms Champions.' *INSEAD* (blog). https://knowledge.insead.edu/blog/insead-blog/jacinda-ardern-and-andrew-cuomo-are-crisis-comms-champions-14006.

360 Connexion. How Did Procter & Gamble Come Out of the Great Depression. https://360connexion.com/article/how-did-procter-gamble-come-out-of-the-great-depression/ (accessed on 6 June 2020).

CHAPTER 2

Farnam Street (FS). 2017. 'Under One Roof: What Can We Learn from the Mayo Clinic?' https://fs.blog/2017/01/under-one-roof-what-can-we-learn-from-the-mayo-clinic/.

Gopalakrishnan, R., and Pallavi Mody. 2020. *How Anil Naik Built L&T's Remarkable Growth Trajectory*, 87. New Delhi: Rupa Publications India.

Knowledge@Wharton (blog). 2018, 28 August. 'How the Mayo Clinic Built Its Reputation as a Top Hospital.' University of Pennsylvania. https://knowledge.wharton.upenn.edu/article/mayo-clinics-secret-success/ (accessed on 6 June 2020).

Kotter, John. 1999. *What Leaders Really Do?* 53. Brighton: The Harvard Business Review Book.

Sandberg, Sheryl. 2013. *Lean In: Women, Work and the Will to Lead.* New York, NY: Random House Group Limited.

Slaughter, Annie. 2013, 7 March. 'Yes, You Can.' *New York Times.* https://www.nytimes.com/2013/03/10/books/review/sheryl-sandbergs-lean-in.html (accessed on 1 June 2020).

CHAPTER 3

Alex's Lemonade Stand Foundation. n.d. 'Alexandra "Alex" Scott Biography.' https://www.alexslemonade.org/alexandra-alex-scott-biography.

Chatterjee, Debashis. 2012. *Timeless Leadership: 18 Leadership Sutras from the Bhagvad Gita.* Singapore: John Wiley & Sons Pvt Ltd.

Creswell, Julie. 2018, 6 August. 'Indra Nooyi, PepsiCo C.E.O. Who Pushed for Healthier Products, to Step Down.' *New York Times.* https://www.nytimes.com/2018/08/06/business/indra-nooyi-pepsi.html (accessed 11 June 2020).

Denning, Steve. 2011, 25 July. The Four Stories You Need to Lead Deep Organizational Change. *Forbes Media LLC.* https://www.forbes.com/sites/stevedenning/2011/07/25/the-four-stories-you-need-to-lead-deep-organizational-change/#3869695353b2 (accessed on 9 June 2020).

Duckworth, Angela. 2019. *Grit: Why Passion and Persistence Are the Secrets to Success*, 173 London: Penguin Random House UK.

Gruber, Manuel. 2018, 1 October. 'Nipun Mehta: Changing the World through Generosity.' *Dreama TV* (blog). http://www.dreama.tv/2018/10/nipun-mehta-changing-the-world-through-generosity/ .

Haviland, E. 2018, 19 March. Wikipedia: The Ultimate Crowdsourced Knowledge Tool. *HBS—Digital Innovation and Transformation.* https://digital.hbs.edu/platform-digit/submission/wikipedia-the-ultimate-crowdsourced-knowledge-tool/ (accessed on 29 May 2020).

Heifetz, Ronald A., and Marty Linsky. 2002. *Leadership on the Line: Staying Alive through the Dangers of Leading.* Boston, MA: Harvard Business School Press.

Nye, Joseph. 2005. *Soft Power: The Means to Success in World Politics.* New York, NY: PublicAffairs.

Srivastava, Akansha. 2017, 17 April. 'You Hire Professionals for Expertise. If You Have Hired a Creative Agency, Then Give Them Independence: Amul's RS Sodhi.' *Best Media Info.* 17 April 2017. https://bestmediainfo.com/2017/04/you-hire-professionals-for-expertise-if-you-have-hired-a-creative-agency-then-give-them-independence-amul-rsquo-s-rs-sodhi/ (accessed on 29 May 2020).

YS Community. 2016, 19 September. 'The Utterly Butterly Delicious Story of Amul.' *YourStory Media Pvt Ltd.* https://yourstory.com/2016/09/the-story-behind-amul?utm_pageloadtype=scrollhttps://yourstory.com/2016/09/the-story-behind-amul?utm_pageloadtype=scroll

CHAPTER 4

Arnette, Greg. 2018, 13 September. Disrupt Yourself—Or Someone Else Will. *Entrepreneur India.* https://www.entrepreneur.com/article/319764 (accessed on 2 July 2020).

Aurik, Johan. 2018, 19 January. 'Why Automation, Not Augmentation Is Needed in Leadership.' *World Economic Forum*. https://www.weforum.org/agenda/2018/01/the-case-for-automating-leadership/.

Fux, Eldad. 2019, 1 December. 'The Most Important Things I Learned as a CTO and a Technology Leader.' *Medium* (blog). https://medium.com/better-programming/the-most-important-things-i-learned-as-a-cto-and-a-technology-leader-511ecfc4d840.

Harris, Tristan. 2016, 19 May. 'How Technology is Hijacking Your Mind—from a Magician and Google Design Ethicist.' *Medium* (blog). https://medium.com/thrive-global/how-technology-hijacks-peoples-minds-from-a-magician-and-google-s-design-ethicist-56d62ef5edf3.

Hidalgo, Nitza. 1993. 'Multicultural teacher introspection.' In *Freedom's Plow: Teaching in the Multicultural Classroom*, edited by T. Perry and J. Fraser. New York, NY: Routledge.

Hughes, Richard, Robert Ginnett, and Gordon Curphy. 2013. *Leadership: Enhancing the Lessons of Experience*. New York, NY: McGraw-Hill Irwin.

Levine, Rick, Christopher Locke, Doc Searls, and David Weinberger. 2000. *The Cluetrain Manifesto*. Cambridge, MA: Perseus Books.

McCrum, Dan. 2018, 4 July. 'Intel's Disruption, and the Problem with Every Token Pitch.' *Financial Times*. https://ftalphaville.ft.com/2018/07/04/1530708299000/Intel-s-disruption--and-the-problem-with-every-token-pitch/ (accessed on 2 July 2020).

Quotes. 'Business is a good game....' https://www.quotes.net/quote/35800 (accessed on 6 July 2020).

Sagar, Ram. 2020, 14 May. Intel Goes Heavy on Disruption, Invests $132 M in 11 AI Startups. *Analytics India Magazine.* https://analyticsindiamag.com/intel-capital-investment-startups-ai/ (accessed on 3 July 2020).

Segal, Leerom, Aaron Goldstein, Jay Goldman, and Rahaf Harfoush. 2014. *The Decoded Company: Know Your Talent Better Than You Know Your Customers.* New York, NY: Penguin Group.

Wikipedia. 2020, 10 June. 'Gustave Eiffel.' https://en.wikipedia.org/wiki/Gustave_Eiffel (accessed on 6 July 2020).

CHAPTER 5

Churchill, Winston. 1940, 13 May. 'Blood, Toil, Tears and Sweat'. Speech, International Churchill Society, 1940, May 13. https://winstonchurchill.org/resources/speeches/1940-the-finest-hour/blood-toil-tears-and-sweat-2/

Newport, Cal. 2016. *Deep Work: Rules for Focused Success in a Distracted World.* London: Piatkus Little, Brown Book Group.

Stahl, Ashley. 2020, 15 June. What Does Covid-19 Mean for the Future of Work? *Forbes.* https://www.forbes.com/sites/ashleystahl/2020/06/15/what-does-covid-19-mean-for-the-future-of-work/#409e8384446f (accessed on 28 July 2020).

PART II

CHAPTER 6

Barker, Joel Arthur. 1922. *Future Edge: Discovering the New Paradigms of Success.* New York, NY: W. Morrow.

Bryner, Andy, and Dawna Markova. 1996. *An Unused Intelligence: Physical Thinking for 21st Century Leadership.* Berkeley, CA: Conari Press.

Chatterjee, Debashis. 1998. *Leading Consciously: A Pilgrimage toward Self-Mastery.* New York, NY: Butterworth-Heinemann.

Chopra, Deepak. 1989. *Quantum Healing: Exploring the Frontiers of Mind/Body Science.* New York, NY: Bantam Books.

———. 1994. *The Seven Spiritual Laws of Success: A Practical Guide to the Fulfillment of Your Dreams.* Novato, Calif: Amber-Allen Publishing and New World Library.

Greenleaf, Robert K. 1977. *Servant Leadership: A Journey into the Nature of Legitimate Power and Greatness.* New York, NY: Paulist Press.

Hebert V. Guenther, and Leslie S. Kawamura, trans. 1975. Tshe-mchog-gliṅ Ye-śes-rgyal-mtshan, *Mind in Buddhist Psychology.* Tibetan translation series. Emeryville, CA: Dharma Publishing.

Jalāl al-Dīn Rūmī. 1995. *The Essential Rumi.* Translated by Coleman Barks. New York, NY: Harper Collins.

Senge, Peter M. 1990. *The Fifth Discipline: The Art and Practice of the Learning Organization.* New York, NY: Doubleday/Currency.

Sobel, Jyoti, Prem Sobel, Aurobindo Ghose, and Mother. 1991. *The Hierarchy of Minds: The Mind Levels: A Compilation from the Works of Sri Aurobindo and the Mother.* Pondicherry: Sri Aurobindo Ashram Publications Department.

Yuasa, Yasuo, Shigenori Nagatomo, and Monte S. Hull. 1993. *The Body, Self-Cultivation, and Ki-Energy.* SUNY series, the body in culture, history, and religion. Albany, NY: State University of New York Press.

CHAPTER 7

Asimov, Isaac, and Bill Barss. 1959. *Words of Science and the History behind Them*. New York, NY: New American Library.

Bstan-Dzin-Rgya-Mtsho, Dalai Lama, and Donald S. Lopez. 1995. *The Way to Freedom: Core Teachings of Tibetan Buddhism*. The Path to Enlightenment Series. New Delhi: Harper Collins.

Campbell, Joseph. 1968. *The Masks of God: Creative Mythology*. New York, NY: Viking Press.

Capra, Fritjof. 1975. *The Tao of Physics: An Exploration of the Parallels between Modern Physics and Eastern Mysticism*. Berkeley, CA: Shambhala Publications.

———. 1988. *Uncommon Wisdom: Conversations with Remarkable People*. New York, NY: Simon & Schuster.

———. 1996. *The Web of Life: A New Scientific Understanding of Living Systems*. New York, NY: Anchor Books.

Chatterjee, Debashis. 1998. *Leading Consciously: A Pilgrimage toward Self-Mastery*. New York, NY: Butterworth-Heinemann.

Mahadevan, T. M. P. *1989. Talks with Sri Ramana Maharshi*. Tiruvannamalai: Sri Ramanasramam.

Merrell-Wolff, Franklin. 1973. *The Philosophy of Consciousness Without an Object: Reflections on the Nature of Transcendental Consciousness*. New York, NY: Julian Press.

Ornstein, Robert E. 1977. *The Psychology of Consciousness*. New York: Harcourt Brace Jovanovich.

Plato. 1953. *The Dialogues of Plato*. Oxford: Clarendon Press.

Pyarelal. 1956. *Mahatma Gandhi: The Early Phase*. Ahmedabad: Navajivan.

KARMA SUTRAS

Ranganathananda, Swami, and Elva Linnéa Nelson. 1991. *Human Being in Depth: A Scientific Approach to Religion*. Albany, NY: State University of New York Press.

Sherman, Stratford. 1996, April–May. 'Leadership Can Be Learnt', *Span*.

Welch Jr., John F. 1990, 26 March. Today's Leaders Look to Tomorrow: Managing John F. Welch Jr. We've Got to Simplify and Delegate More. *Fortune Magazine*.

CHAPTER 8

Aurobindo, Sri. 1977. *The Message of the Gita*. Pondicherry: Sri Aurobindo Ashram.

Boldt, Laurence G. 1996. *How to Find the Work You Love*. New York: Arkana.

Chatterjee, Debashis. 1998. *Leading Consciously: A Pilgrimage toward Self-Mastery*. New York, NY: Butterworth-Heinemann.

Chatterjee, Debashis. 2008. *Leadership Sutras: A Pilgrimage toward Self-Mastery*. New Delhi: Elsevier.

Jalāl al-Dīn Rūmī. 1995. *The Essential Rumi*. Translated by Coleman Barks. New York: Harper Collins.

Lindbergh, Charles A. 1978. *Autobiography of Values*. New York: Harcourt Brace Jovanovich.

Mother Teresa, and Angelo Devananda. 1985. *Total Surrender*. Ann Arbor, MI: Servant Publications.

Robertson, Roland. 1992. *Globalization: Social Theory and Global Culture*. London: SAGE Publications.

Sobel, Jyoti, Prem Sobel, Aurobindo Ghose, and Mother. 1991. *The Hierarchy of Minds: The Mind Levels: A Compilation from the Works of Sri Aurobindo and the Mother*. Pondicherry: Sri Aurobindo Ashram Publications Department.

Stark, Eleanor. 1988. *The Gift Unopened: A New American Revolution*. Portsmouth: P.E. Randall.

Wilson, Andrew, ed. 1993. *World Scripture: A Comparative Anthology of Sacred Texts*. New Delhi: Motilal Banarsidas.

CHAPTER 9

Cannon, Walter B. 1963. *The Wisdom of the Body*. New York, NY: W.W. Norton.

Chatterjee, Debashis. 1998. *Leading Consciously: A Pilgrimage toward Self-Mastery*. New York, NY: Butterworth-Heinemann.

Fischer, Louis, ed. 1962. *The Essential Gandhi: His Life, Work, and Ideas: An Anthology*. New York, NY: Vintage Books.

Jacobi, Jolande Székács, ed. 1969. *Paracelsus: Selected Writings*. Bollingen Series, 28. Princeton, NJ: Princeton University Press.

Krishnamurti, J. 1994. *On Learning and Knowledge*. New York: Harper Collins.

Mother Teresa, and Angelo Devananda. 1985. *Total Surrender*. Ann Arbor, MI: Servant Publications.

Remde, Harry. 1975. *The Art in a Craft*. Toronto: Traditional Studies Press.

Renesch, John, ed. 1991. *New Traditions in Business: Spirit and Leadership in the 21st Century*. San Francisco, CA: Sterling and Stone.

Senge, Peter M. 1990. *The Fifth Discipline: The Art and Practice of the Learning Organization*. New York, NY: Doubleday/Currency.

Tagore, Rabindranath. 1955. *Fireflies*. New York: Macmillan.

Williams, Charles. 1965. *The Place of the Lion*. Grand Rapids, MI: William B. Eerdmans.

CHAPTER 10

Abram, David. 1996. *The Spell of the Sensuous: Perception and Language in a More-Than-Human World*. New York: Pantheon Books.

Aurobindo, Sri, and Mother. 1973. *On Self-Perfection*. Pondicherry: Sri Aurobindo Ashram.

———. 1983, August. *Parabola Myth and the Quest for Meaning. Words of Power. Volume VIII, Number 3*. New York, NY: Society for the Study of Myth and Tradition,.

Chatterjee, Debashis. 1998. *Leading Consciously: A Pilgrimage Toward Self-Mastery*. New York, NY: Butterworth-Heinemann.

Jalāl al-Dīn Rūmī. *The Essential Rumi*. Translated by Coleman Barks. New York, NY: Harper Collins, 1995.

Krishnamurti, J. 1994. *On Learning and Knowledge*. New York, NY: Harper Collins.

Mahadevan, T. M. P. *1989. Talks with Sri Ramana Maharshi*. Tiruvannamalai: Sri Ramanasramam.

Mother Teresa, and Angelo Devananda. 1985. *Total Surrender*. Ann Arbor, MI: Servant Publications.

Shakespeare, William. 2008. *Hamlet*. Edited by George Richard Hibbard. New York: Oxford University Press.

Swarup, Ram. 1980. *The Word as Revelation: Names of God*. New Delhi: Impex India.

CHAPTER 11

Bstan-Dzin-Rgya-Mtsho, Dalai Lama, and Donald S. Lopez. 1995. *The Way to Freedom. Core Teachings of Tibetan Buddhism*. The Path to Enlightenment Series. New Delhi: Harper Collins.

Chakraborty, S. K. 1993. *Management by Values: Towards Cultural Congruence*. New Delhi: Oxford University Press.

Chan, Wing-tsit. 1963. *A Source Book in Chinese Philosophy*. Princeton, NJ: Princeton University Press.

Chatterjee, Debashis. 1998. *Leading Consciously: A Pilgrimage toward Self-Mastery*. New York, NY: Butterworth-Heinemann.

Chatterjee, Debashis. 2016, 12 July. 'Takers, Givers, Matchers: Science of Happiness!' LinkedIn. https://www.linkedin.com/pulse/takers-givers-matchers-science-happiness-debashis-chatterjee/

Chatterjee, Debashis. 2017, 23 January. 'Change!' LinkedIn. https://www.linkedin.com/pulse/change-debashis-chatterjee/.

Fischer, Louis, ed. 1962. *The Essential Gandhi: His Life, Work, and Ideas: An Anthology*. New York, NY: Vintage Books.

Fukuyama, Francis. 1992. *The End of History and the Last Man*. New York, NY: Avon.

Gibran, Kahlil. 1970. *The Prophet*. New York: Alfred A. Knopf.

Griggs, Lewis Brown, and Lente-Louise Louw, eds. 1995. *Valuing Diversity: New Tools for a New Reality*. New York: McGraw-Hill.

Kurien, V. 1978. *Managing Socio-Economic Change: The Role of Professionals*. Ahmedabad: Indian Institute of Management Publication.

Pollar, Odette, and Rafael González. 1994. *Dynamics of Diversity: Strategic Programs for Your Organization*. Menlo Park, CA: Crisp Publications.

Russell, Bertrand. 1931. *The Scientific Outlook*. London: George Allen & Unwin.

Saint-Exupéry, Antoine de. 1971. *The Little Prince*. Translated from French by Katherine Woods. New York: Harcourt Brace Jovanovich.

 KARMA SUTRAS

Senge, Peter M. 1990. *The Fifth Discipline: The Art and Practice of the Learning Organization*. New York: Doubleday/Currency.

Walsh, James. 1993, 14 June. 'Asia's Different Drum'. *Time*.

CHAPTER 12

Chatterjee, Debashis. 1998. *Leading Consciously: A Pilgrimage toward Self-Mastery*. New York, NY: Butterworth-Heinemann.

Chatterjee, Debashis. 2015, 11 July. 'Small Work, Great Love!' LinkedIn. https://www.linkedin.com/pulse/small-work-great-love-debashis-chatterjee/

Chopra, Deepak. 1997. *The Path to Love: Spiritual Lessons for Creating the Love You Need*. New York: Rider Books.

Gibran, Kahlil. 1970. *The Prophet*. New York, NY: Alfred A. Knopf.

Krishnamurti, J. 1994. *On Learning and Knowledge*. New York, NY: Harper Collins.

Moir, Anne, and David Jessel. 1989. *Brainsex: The Real Difference between Men and Women*. New York, NY: Dell Publishing.

Mother Teresa, and Angelo Devananda. 1985. *Total Surrender*. Ann Arbor, MI: Servant Publications.

Wilhelm, Richard, and H. G. Oswald, trans. 1995. *Lao Tzu*. New York: Penguin Books.

CHAPTER 13

Chatterjee, Debashis. 1998. *Leading Consciously: A Pilgrimage toward Self-Mastery*. New York, NY: Butterworth-Heinemann.

Daumal, Rene. 1988, November. *Mount Analogue*, quoted in *Parabola*.

Fischer, Louis, ed. 1962. *The Essential Gandhi: His Life, Work, and Ideas: An Anthology*. New York, NY: Vintage Books.

Frawley, David. 1992. *Wisdom of the Ancient Seers: Mantras of the Rig Veda*. Salt Lake City, Utah: Passage Press.

Hughes, Holly, and Mark Weakley. 1994. *Meditations on the Earth: A Celebration of Nature, in Quotations, Poems, and Essays*. Philadelphia, PA: Running Press.

Krishnamurti, J. 1994. *On Learning and Knowledge*. New York: Harper Collins.

Mother Teresa, and Angelo Devananda. 1985. *Total Surrender*. Ann Arbor, MI: Servant Publications.

Tagore, Rabindranath. 1955. *Fireflies*. New York: Macmillan.

Thoreau, Henry David, and Arthur G. Volkman. 1960. *Thoreau on Man and Nature*. New York, NY: Peter Pauper Press.

CHAPTER 14

Chatterjee, Debashis. 1998. *Leading Consciously: A Pilgrimage toward Self-Mastery*. New York, NY: Butterworth-Heinemann.

Chatterjee, Debashis. 2008. *Leadership Sutras: A Pilgrimage toward Self-Mastery*. New Delhi: Elsevier.

Mother Teresa, and Angelo Devananda. 1985. *Total Surrender*. Ann Arbor, MI: Servant Publications.

Radhakrishnan, Sarvepalli. 1956. *Mahatma Gandhi: Essays and Reflections on His Life and Work, Presented to Him on His Seventieth Birthday, October 2nd, 1939; Together with a New Memorial Section*. Bombay: Jaico Publishing House.

Smith, Houston. 1991. *The World's Religions: Our Great Wisdom Traditions*. New York, NY: Harper.